DISCOVERING
PREHISTORIC ROCK ART

DISCOVERING PREHISTORIC ROCK ART

A RECORDING MANUAL

KAY KENADY SANGER and CLEMENT W. MEIGHAN

Wormwood Press
Calabasas, California

Copyright 1990 © by Wormwood Press
P.O. Box 8125, Calabasas, California 91372

Library of Congress Cataloging in Publication Data:
Sanger, Kay.
    Discovering Prehistoric Rock Art : A Recording Manual / Kay Kenady
Sanger and Clement W. Meighan. — 1st ed.
        240 pp. 18 by 25.5 cm.
        Bibliography: 11 p.
        ISBN 0-937523-03-8 : $22.95
        1. Rock paintings—handbooks, manuals, etc. 2. Petroglyphs—
handbooks, manuals, etc. I. Meighan, Clement Woodward, 1925-
II. Title.
GN799.P4S14 1990
930.1'028—dc19

                                        88-38319 CIP

Printed in the United States of America
First Edition

CONTENTS

FOREWORD
Frank Bock

...Listen to the tale
Of human suffering, and how at first
Senseless as Beasts, I gave men sense, possessed them
Of mind...
I do but tell of good gifts I conferred...
Moreover, number the most excellent
Of all inventions, I for them devised,
And gave them writing that retaineth all....

Aeschylus, Prometheus Bound

The legendary Prometheus, having brought to mankind such diverse gifts as knowledge of constructing dwellings, cures for diseases, and the ability to produce fire, listed as the greatest gift of all, the gift of writing. Being capable of recording thoughts in a permanent form was paramount in humanity's cultural progress. This artifact of human endeavor, reflecting all men's heritage, has long caught the attention of archaeologists and historians world wide.

Yet one significant area of recorded "messages" remains unsolved. This is the spectrum of petroglyphs and pictographs, those symbols commonly called "rock art," found carved or painted around the globe—on cave walls, rock cliffs, or isolated boulders. This is not to intimate that rock art is a form of "writing" in the sense of expressing the spoken language, but rather a visible manifestation of the desire for early man to communicate some message in a tangible and permanent manner. No item in the archaeologist's history book is quite so enigmatic as these designs, frozen in perpetuity, and constantly eluding decipherment.

All of us have inherited a legacy left by prehistoric people. In America, the diverging cultures that first peopled this continent spread their influence from mountain to prairie, ocean to ocean. They left remnants of their existence in cliff dwellings and in great cities, in small villages and myriad forms of material culture. Mostly, they left a personal imprint on the succeeding generations. A significant part of this legacy is reflected in their rock art. Not only is this a visible segment of their material culture, this facet also reflects, in most areas, the only viable form of symbolic communication developed by these early cultures.

It is therefore most important that rock art be located and recorded, to continue to be a valuable addition to the archaeological data bank—our only source of historical information for prehistoric peoples. This is especially true in the face of steady, absolute, and inevitable destruction of this priceless heritage—both by nature's relentless force, and mankind's perversity.

Rock art is not confined to any geographic location. Thousands of sites are found in Europe, Africa, Asia, Australia, North and South America, and islands dotting the seas. Considering a single design as an element, it means that literally millions of rock art elements exist as forerunners of Prometheus' finest gift. The plethora of rock art has prompted individuals to explore the continents and spawned large groups of people seeking to record and study these designs.

Currently the American Rock Art Research Association, established in 1974, is the leading organization devoted to the study, protection, and conservation of American Indian rock art. Additional groups in the Western Hemisphere include the Canadian Rock Art Research Associates, the Simposium Internacional de Arte Rupestre Americano, Sociedad de Investigacion del Arte Rupestre de Bolivia, and the American Committee to Advance the Study of Petroglyphs and Pictographs. Numerous other organizations, mostly attached to regional universities and museums, also spend considerable time in rock art research.

In Europe, rock art has long been recognized as a significant artifact, and organizations such as the Centro Camuno di Studi Preistorici in Valcamonica, Italy, are testament to that importance. Various groups in Africa, as well as the comparatively new Australian Rock Art Research Association, add even further credence to the world-wide place of rock art study in the annals of archaeology.

So much international emphasis on this study gives substance to Hobbes' admonition that the "...invention of [writing] is a profitable invention for continuing the memory of the past, and the conjunction of mankind dispersed into so many and distant regions of the earth." If in truth we are bound together in this world by our humanity, then doubtlessly rock art remains one of the most enduring forms of that bonding.

This volume of Discovering Prehistoric Rock Art is an important contribution to the field of archaeology. There is a critical need for such an organized approach to methodology in rock art recording. The excitement that grips the heart and mind of anyone who, by chance or by design, comes upon a rock art site, has too often been shattered by a deep feeling of frustration, brought on by the question, "What do I do now.?" Because here you stand, not in some museum gazing at artifacts entombed in glass and out of context, but rather on the very sand that received the footprints of the rock art's originator. You are in his environment, a spontaneous link with the past. And you want to record the moment. Discovering Rock Art will offer the reader a unique opportunity: a systematic and easily understood method of recording that moment that transcends time, whether you have an hour or a month. This overdue, much-needed volume is a significant step forward in our universal desire to see that the world's rock art does not go the way of other ancient cultural resources that have disappeared without a trace.

It is written in the Acknowledgments that this work has been a collaborative effort. Indeed, the present-day rock art researcher owes a debt to the pioneering efforts of Mallery and Steward, to the unsung archaeologists, and to the unknown back-country hiker with his Kodak. In short, this collaboration has been taking place for decades, perhaps centuries if we include Herodotus! Authors and collaborators of this volume have pulled together the thoughts of many, born in the fire of field work and tempered on the anvil of time. Any rock art researcher, from the casual visitor to the professional, will find that the whys and how-tos of this volume are essential, contributing steps that one can take on this continuum of rock art study.

INTRODUCTION

Rock art, the visual remnant of prehistoric and ethnohistoric human culture found carved and painted on rock surfaces throughout the world, holds a fascination for human beings everywhere. It is tangible evidence that earlier peoples were impelled to make their mark and leave artistic and symbolic records behind. We can still appreciate these records today, even though they were produced by peoples whose way of life was totally different from our own and who did not intend for us to see or understand the art.

There are thousands of examples of diverse rock art found in all parts of the world. Yet despite their numbers they are a fragile and non-renewable part of our human heritage that is rapidly being destroyed by the forces of nature and by the actions of contemporary peoples. Rain and wind erode paintings. Thoughtless vandals emblazon their names over exquisite panels. Still others use the art for target practice or try to remove it for private collections. Increasing land development and dam construction have caused further, often unknowing destruction.

Although rock art is a part of the archaeological record of the past, the art is far more subject to destruction than buried remains because it is above ground where it is visible. For this reason, it is disappearing at an alarming rate. Some sites have been entirely destroyed. Others that have been documented over the years show fading, weathering, and vandalism.

Fortunately, there is a bright side to the picture. Not only are there organizations and archives devoted to the preservation of rock art, but also many sites are being safeguarded in parks and monuments. Further, there is increasing awareness and interest among the general public. Many people have made an avocation of discovering and documenting ancient rock art, a hobby which combines the thrill of discovery with the satisfaction of making a contribution to scientific knowledge. Since this can be done at very little expense and without requiring a great deal of technical background or training, it is attractive to those who love the outdoors and are fascinated by the art left behind by vanished peoples. This is one of few scientific areas where it is possible for an individual, working alone, to make important scholarly contributions which are simply incidental to the enjoyment of an exciting avocation. It is no accident that much of the documentation of rock art has come from the "amateurs." The Archive of Prehistoric Rock Art at UCLA has 45 volumes containing thousands of pages of records and photographs on the rock art of Baja California, collected by V. L. Pontoni and her friends, entirely without research grants, institutional sponsorship, or any of the resources of organized science. The same archive has 58 folders of site records and 22 volumes of careful reporting from Paul P. Steed, a Texas recorder who has patiently documented dozens of sites throughout the western United States with written records and thousands of photographs. These are just two examples of many significant contributions to the rock art record made by individuals working on their own and for the fun of it.

It helps to have some advice on how to proceed. This manual provides a practical guide for recording rock art. It is intended to be a "how-to" book, long on specific suggestions and short on theory, discussion, and speculation. While this manual does not pretend to be the final word on the subject, it offers a compilation of rock art recording methods which have been developed and used around the globe. It is aimed at that large number of people who *discover* rock art sites, or who visit rock art sites and feel the urge to get closer to the details and elements revealed. It is intended to help organize the art, and to develop a deeper appreciation and understanding of these "messages from the past." Beginners can learn to record a site, and practicing archaeologists may also profit from these guidelines because this kind of archaeological recording is less known and practiced than conventional excavation.

In addition to this manual, several booklets and articles have been written on the subject of recording rock art. Interested readers are directed in particular to Anati (1977), Apostolides (1975), Bain (1975), Breschini and Haversat (1983), Clewlow and Wheeling (1978), Fenenga (1949), Loendorf , Olsen and Conner (1988), and Pohorecky (1966, 1967). Important general references on rock art in North America are Grant (1967), Mallery (1893 and 1896), and Wellmann (1979).

This manual presents an "ideal" plan for making a total record of a rock art site. However, as with all research, it is not often possible to accomplish everything, particularly at the time of an initial discovery or an unexpected find. A large site may require repeated visits over a long period of time, and it is usually necessary to do the study in phases, proceeding from preliminary recording to more detailed analysis as time permits. One should not conclude that unless every step discussed in this book can be accomplished, it is not worth compiling a partial record. A recorder can make valuable observations and notes even during a casual visit of an hour or two. A major expedition is not always needed, and much can be completed without a great deal of technical background or equipment. You need only your powers of observation, a pencil, and a piece of paper to make a preliminary record. If you have a camera, take some pictures. You don't *have* to have two cameras, three lenses, and a collection of photographic filters. Any picture is better than no picture—any record is better than no record at all.

The following chapters recognize the need for a series of phases in the recording effort. They attempt to point out what should be done first so the work can proceed to greater and greater detail. Obviously, no iron-clad set of rules can be given since all sites are different and the circumstances of recording also are extremely variable.

Beginners are sometimes reluctant to launch into an effort at documenting a rock art site because they can't believe that the site isn't already known and recorded, particularly if it happens to be in a city park where generations of local people have gone for picnics. *Yet many of these sites, even the best-known, have never been scientifically recorded so they are essentially "undiscovered."* Scientific discovery belongs to the person who makes the scientific record. Dozens of new rock art discoveries are made every year because interested people choose to document them rather than give the location a passing glance and go on their way. A careful investigator will often find undiscovered elements and relationships at sites which have already been recorded and published.

The time to begin some kind of a record is the first time you see a site. Don't assume that the site will be there next year, or next week for that matter. One well-known archaeologist made that mistake. He made three visits to a rock art site in Mexico and managed to put off recording it because the rock art (including some very well done images of jaguars) was high off the ground on a granite boulder about the size of a house. It appeared safe and indestructible. However, some of the local people decided this giant rock with the images marked the location of buried treasure, so at great trouble and expense they carted in a case of dynamite and blew the rock to smithereens. Except for a couple of inadequate photos, there is no record today that this site ever existed.

Even if disasters of this magnitude do not happen, sites can be counted upon to deteriorate or disappear due to natural causes. Every record must be considered an urgent necessity. If there is satisfaction in doing the recording, there is certainly a greater reward in having made the only record that can ever be made of a rock art location the way it looks today.

Sample forms for recording rock art are provided in Appendix B. These are designed to be photocopied, taken into the field where they can be completed, and then copied again to be sent to an appropriate repository of archaeological information.

Because of its practical emphasis, this manual contains no comprehensive list of references, although the bibliography provides the key general publications as well as a list of regional studies in North America. Very detailed bibliographies listing rock art studies are found in numerous summary volumes. For example, the survey of North American rock art by Wellmann (1979) has over 1000 references to published rock art studies. Similar comprehensive bibliographies are available for such widely separated locations as Argentina and Australia.

1

VARIETIES OF ROCK ART

Rock art is a term referring primarily to carvings and paintings made by aboriginal peoples on natural rock surfaces. It also includes images made by scraping away gravel or earth from the surface of the ground to reveal the underlying soil, as well as placing rocks in patterned arrangements on the ground. Some rock art is found almost everywhere that rock surfaces are exposed, and it is absent only in areas of alluvium where no rocks with useable surfaces are to be found. Desert areas are particularly favored for rock art since there is plenty of exposed rock and little vegetation to cover it. Rock art also is found along jungle rivers and in heavily forested areas, on rocks along the ocean shore and at the top of mountain peaks (figs. 1-1 to 1-6).

Most rock art is prehistoric and beyond the memory of living people, but in a few places rock art is still being produced by native peoples. There is often a native oral history which gives clues to the meaning of the art, and may even name the individuals of previous generations who produced the art.

A rock art site may consist of only one nondescript image or an assemblage of hundreds of images. It may occur on huge cliffs or in hidden caves; on large boulders or small moveable rocks. It may have been created in plain view, either in the middle of a native village or displayed where it could be seen from a great distance. Sometimes it was placed in a

1-1 Gardner Cave, central Baja California.

1-2 Petroglyphs on exposed basalt cliff face, Mono County, California. Photo ca. 1956.

1-3 Boulder field, site Riv-114, Riverside County, California. Paintings occur in the crevice between two boulders (arrow) and on several others of the large granite boulders at this location. Photo Joan Seibert, 1981.

1-4 *The Indian God Rock Petroglyphs site (36 VE-26), Pennsylvania, on a large sloping rock next to river. Photo W. C. Reeves, 1962.*

1-5 *Pictograph location on ceiling of small rock shelter at Exeter Rocky Hill, Tulare County, California. Photo 1982.*

1-6 *Petroglyphs on isolated boulder, Coso rock art site, California. In some locations rock art of this kind is on rocks small enough to be picked up, resulting in loss of as much as 30% of the elements at a given site due to the rock art being carried away by collectors. Photo 1965.*

hidden cave where it was not intended to be seen by everyone. Despite the variety of rock art sites, there were only three basic techniques used to make the art.

THE MAJOR TECHNIQUES USED TO CREATE ROCK ART

- **PICTOGRAPHS:**   Painted figures on rock surfaces (figs. 1-7 to 1-9).

- **PETROGLYPHS:**   Figures impressed into the surfaces by pecking, scraping, or making grooves with stone tools (figs. 1-10 to 1-15).

- **GROUND FIGURES:** Two main varieties:
  Intaglios or Geoglyphs: Figures, often very large, produced by removing rocks and/or earth to expose the contrasting color of the underlying soil. Individual figures may be more than 100 feet long; groups may cover a whole hillside (figs. 1-32 to 1-34).
  Rock alignments: Figures formed by rocks and boulders on the ground surface, mostly linear or circular forms.

Each of these terms is further defined on the following pages. Some areas have many different kinds of rock art, and in some locations there are both pictographs and petroglyphs in the same site. Some desert areas may have all of the above kinds of rock art in a very small region of only a few square miles. Some peoples produced multiple kinds of rock art, but varieties of rock art in the same place may not mean that they were produced by the same people or at the same time.

PICTOGRAPHS

Pictograph is the common American term for rock paintings. Some scholars prefer to use "petroglyph" (rock picture) as a term which includes both painted and carved rock art. In painted rock art, the most common colors are black, white, and red, used either singly or in combination.

1-7 *Pictographs on sandstone ledge. Edgar Rock, San Luis Obispo County, California. Photo Joan Seibert, 1980.*

1-8 *Life-size paintings of deer and mountain sheep above Pajaro Negro shelter in central Baja California, Mexico. Black and red are the colors used. Photo 1962.*

1-9 *Pictographs in small shelter, San Diego County, California. Photo 1976.*

1-10 Petroglyphs of human hands chipped into basaltic rock surface, McCoy Peak near Blythe, California. Petroglyphs of human hands and feet are found world-wide. Photo 1982.

1-11 Petroglyphs made by incising grooves in soft rock. Castle Garden, Wyoming. Photo from Heizer collection, by Dale W. Ritter, 1961.

1-12 Petroglyphs chipped into rock surface; some grooves rubbed with an abrading stone. Bottle Hollow, Utah. Photo 1979.

1-13 Petroglyphs in a burial cave on
Easter Island. Photo Wm. D. Hyder,
1982.

1-14 Petroglyphs in a cave in the Dominican Republic, near La
Descubierta, Independencia Region. Photo Steve Young, 1982.

1-15 Large human figures, pecked on basalt surfaces at Petroglyph Canyon near China Lake, California. The
basaltic rock at this location bears a dark patina which is removed in the process of making the petroglyphs, allowing the lighter-colored rock to show and producing a light picture on a dark background—the contrast in
this photo is achieved photographically without use of chalk or other enhancement of the petroglyphs. Photo
1953.

COMMON PIGMENTS USED FOR PICTOGRAPHS

- *Black:* most commonly charcoal, sometimes manganese oxide.
- *White:* any chalky rock (including chalk, soft limestone, diatomaceous earth or solidified volcanic ash) or sometimes white ash from wood fires.
- *Red:* usually derived from red ocher (hematite or iron oxide), a near-universal natural pigment found in many soils. Rarely, red pigment was obtained from cinnabar.

LESS COMMON COLORS

- *Yellow:* limonite
- *Green:* malachite or copper-rich rocks
- *Blue:* azurite

Paints were prepared by grinding the pigment to a powder, often on a flat rock (fig. 1-16) or in a small, shallow, stone mortar (not to be confused with mortars used for food preparation, which are generally substantially larger and deeper (fig. 1-17)). Grinding tools with pigment remnants have been found associated with many rock art sites . The paint usually was prepared further by adding some sort of binder such as animal fat, blood, eggs, sap, or oil from seeds. These brought the paint to the proper consistency, and also had a valuable effect in making the painting more permanent. Pigments mixed with a binder have generally survived longer than those applied dry or merely mixed with water.

Paint was applied in a variety of ways. Most aboriginal artists apparently painted with their fingers or hands. Prints of hands dipped in paint are common in many parts of the world (fig. 1-18), as are lines or dots produced by a finger dipped in paint. Sometimes the artists used brushes, made from plant fibers or animal hair. These brushes have been found in a few cave sites containing pictographs. In addition, the artists sometimes used pieces of solid pigment like crayons, particularly with charred sticks or white chalk-like rocks. They also painted with both dry

1-16 Contemporary Australian aborigine producing a rock art panel at the International Rock Art Conference, Darwin, Australia 1988. Powdered paints are ground on the stones in the foreground. The kangaroo is done in "X-ray style" which shows the animal's internal organs; this style is common in northern Australian rock art sites. Photo Joan Seibert, 1988.

1-17 Bedrock mortars adjacent to Exeter Rocky Hill, Tulare County, California. Although these mortars could be used for grinding pigment for rock art, in this size and number they are more likely mortars used in the preparation of plant foods. Smaller bedrock mortars are often found in rock art sites, and in some cases they still contain traces of the pigment that was ground in them. These are to be contrasted with cupules, which are generally much smaller and shallower and rarely occur on horizontal surfaces.

1-18 Pictographs at Riv-114, Riverside County, California. Painted in red, with numerous hand prints (upper right). Photo Daniel McCarthy, 1980.

1-19 Contemporary Australian rock art (see 1-16). Note negative prints of hands, made by spraying paint over hands against the rock (contrast with positive hand prints in fig. 1-18 made by dipping hands in paint and pressing them against the rock). Photo Joan Seibert, 1988.

28

and liquid pigment by blowing it through a tube or spraying a mouthful of paint onto the rock. Sprayed paint was usually applied over a hand or other object on the wall, producing a negative image, of which the most well-known are the negative hand prints found in many locations in the New World, Europe, and Australia (fig. 1-19). Several authors have suggested that this effect could also be produced by using some sort of paint-saturated puff, which could be daubed over the hand or other object to produce a negative image.

Rock paintings are only one use aboriginal peoples made of pigment. They also painted their faces, bodies, clothing and artifacts. While most of the other painted artifacts have not withstood the test of time, it is sometimes possible to relate elements of the rock art to known figures and designs used for body paint or other decorative purposes. The discovery of such parallel uses provides important clues to symbolism and meaning. For example, a design element used to identify membership in a clan, painted on the face or body of clan members, may also occur in rock art and have the same connotation.

Due to fading, weathering, and deposition of soot and grime, rock paintings are not always brightly colored and easy to see. In one case a team of archaeologists excavating a cave site worked in the cave for several weeks before anyone noticed the black pictographs on the wall of the cave. It is easy to overlook many pictographs unless you are consciously seeking them. Some are very apparent, but others are in such an advanced state of deterioration that it may not be possible to make a drawing or photograph clearly showing the rock art. Such situations constitute a real challenge for the recorder. When there is differential weathering, where virtually all of one color has disappeared while other colors still survive, curious effects are produced in which parts of figures may be missing.

PETROGLYPHS

Petroglyphs are carvings on rocks, made most often by direct percussion (pecked with a hammerstone), but occasionally produced by indirect percussion (use of two stones, in the manner of a hammer and chisel). The indirect method allows more precision. Abrasion (rubbing grooves in the rock using other rocks) was another method. Petroglyphs formed by abrasion are usually found on soft surfaces like sandstone or soapstone (fig. 1-20). Sometimes recorders misinterpret random grooves on a stone which may not be rock art at all, but instead are places where bone awls, stone axes, and other tools were ground or sharpened (fig. 1-21).

Occasionally, petroglyphs were enhanced and further emphasized by painting, usually with red, white, or black pigment applied to the pecked or abraded grooves. Recorders of rock art must be cautious in discriminating aboriginal paint on petroglyphs from pigments applied by recent observers. The latter is particularly common with white pigments, which are usually modern chalking (figs. 1-22, 1-23). However, red and black pigments are also occasionally added by contemporary people. Enamel paints are easy to recognize as modern additions, particularly when they are applied in unusual colors like green, which rarely appears in rock art. However, if a dry pigment like chalk or charcoal was used by a recent visitor to the site, it may not be easy to discriminate from pigments applied by ancient artists. Furthermore, in cases of genuine aboriginal painting of petroglyphs, most of the pigment will very likely have disappeared and only faint traces of it will be present, making it easy to overlook and easy to obscure by more recent over-painting.

Sun and moisture cause most rocks (even granite) to form weathered or patinated surfaces which are a different color from the underlying rock. This is most clearly seen in the accumulation of organically derived minerals on the surfaces of many desert rocks, giving them a darker brown, grey, or bluish-black patina that is called "desert varnish." Petroglyphs chipped through such dark patinated surfaces stand out sharply when first made, and elements known to be hundreds of years old may appear visually as light-colored figures on dark backgrounds. In photographs, these petroglyphs look like white figures on black backgrounds (figs. 1-24, 1-25). Over time, however, the desert varnish will build again

1-20 Grooved petroglyph, China Lake, California. Photo 1953. Compare with 1-21.

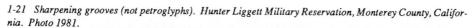

1-21 Sharpening grooves (not petroglyphs). Hunter Liggett Military Reservation, Monterey County, California. Photo 1981.

1-22   Early rock art recording (1890's?) at Smith's Ferry Petroglyphs Site, Pennsylvania. From Carnegie Museum (Pittsburgh); their photo no. 5023. Negative supplied by Harold B. Barth. The unknown lady holds a piece of chalk with which the petroglyphs have been marked. It appears that the area was also dampened with water from the river. Careful study of the photograph suggests that other rock art elements are present but they cannot be made out in the photograph. While chalking is generally considered an improper and potentially dangerous impact on petroglyphs, would we be able to see the elements at all if they were not chalked?

1-23   Petroglyphs of spirals, another universal element which occurs worldwide. Tepic, Nayarit, Mexico. These have also been chalked, although adequate photographs could be obtained without use of chalk.   Photo 1961.

and eventually will darken the petroglyph to the point where it is the same color as the surrounding surface. At this stage, it can be seen only with difficulty, and sometimes is identifiable only by feeling the original pecked marks. In the many cases where rock art was produced on the same rock over a long period of time, it is easy to recognize the older from the more recent elements by their color, showing the degree to which the patination has re-formed since the petroglyph was made (fig. 1-26, 1-27). This is clearly visible in cases of superimposition, where the upper (more recent) element will often be substantially lighter in color than the picture it overlies. Researchers are trying to determine the rate of patination for desert rocks in order to provide absolute ages of the rock art (discussed in the chapter on Dating).

A very inconspicuous form of petroglyph, generally invisible unless the lighting is just right, is produced by fine-line scratches made with a sharp stone flake or perhaps an arrow-point. These are single-stroke marks as thin as a pencil line which, if seen at all, may be interpreted as scarring or natural cracks. Their validity as man-made rock art is confirmed by the appearance of patterns such as mazes or cross-hatching. In this form of rock art, the scratches are very fine and the design elements tend to be quite small, only a few inches in average dimensions. Such small incised elements are often unnoticed even in sites where other rock art is found. In one instance (King, 1981), recognition of such elements provided an undiscovered style of rock art in rock shelters which had long been known for other more visible rock art (fig. 1-28).

1-24   Petroglyphs in Utah. Photo from Heizer collection, original taken by Campbell Grant.

1-25   Petroglyphs at Petrified Forest, northern Arizona. Photo 1986.

1-26   Petroglyphs from China Lake, California. Photo D. Tiemanns, 1954.

1-27   Animal petroglyphs from China Lake, California. Photo D. Tiemanns, 1954.

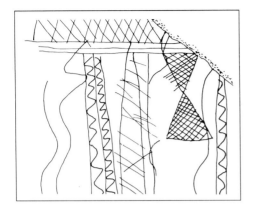 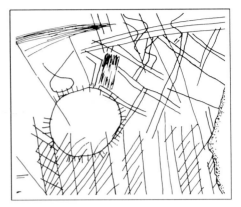

1-28a,b Drawings of incised line petroglyphs. Elements of this style were cut into sandstone with a sharp implement. Individual elements are quite small, less than a few centimeters in height. Drawings after King, 1981.

Cupules. Cupules are a special kind of petroglyph composed of small cup-shaped depressions in rocks, formed by pecking and/or grinding a small pit in the rock surface. Often associated with grooved lines, this type of rock art is often referred to as "pit and groove" style, although many cupule boulders have nothing but small pits. The individual pits are often not much bigger than a fingertip and less than an inch deep, but there may be hundreds of them on a rock (fig. 1-29 to 1-31)

*1-29 Cupules in Arizona. These are larger than most cupules, but are readily distinguishable from bedrock mortars (fig. 1-17) because they are on a sloping surface and are too small for grinding seeds.
Photo Dawn Bergland.*

36

*1-30 A cupule boulder in Riverside County, California. Photo David Van Horn, 1988.
Contrast with 1-17 (bedrock mortars)*

1-31 Cupules in Little Petroglyph Canyon, near China Lake, California. Photo Joan Seibert, 1985.

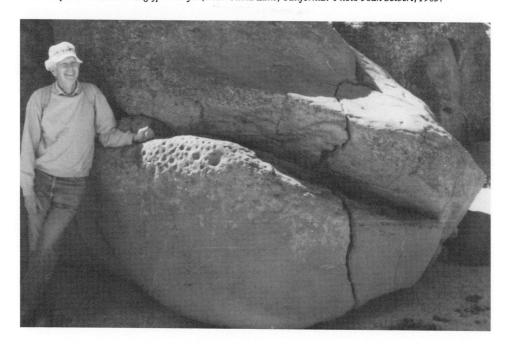

37

Cupules are among the most subtle and frequently overlooked type of petroglyph, although they are found throughout the world. Some indication of how easy it is to overlook these small pitted boulders can be seen in the fact that they have been found in the middle of sites undergoing extensive excavation yet have been missed by the archaeologists digging the site. Unless you have cupules in mind and are looking for them, you aren't likely to notice them.

Throughout the western United States, cupules are most commonly associated with aboriginal village locations and appear to have been known and produced by the general populace. They may be found on both vertical or horizontal surfaces and they sometimes completely cover a small boulder. They commonly occur in association with larger holes used for grinding seeds (bedrock mortars), but this association may be merely a function of both activities occurring on rocks in the village area. Cupules are sometimes found along with other petroglyphs, connected by grooves or having "rays" around them.

GROUND FIGURES
(GEOGLYPHS)

Geoglyphs or intaglios are designs made by scraping away surface soil or gravel to reveal lighter colored surfaces below. Some intaglio designs are very large figures, best seen from a distance. Examples include rocky surfaces of desert areas where the dark stones of the desert pavement were removed to reveal lighter sand (see fig. 1-32), and grassy areas where turf was removed to reveal the underlying chalk, as in England (fig. 1-33). They were made on hillsides visible from a valley floor, or on level ground. They are usually seen most easily from an airplane. Many designs, in fact, have been discovered by fliers. On the ground, it may be difficult to make out the entire geoglyph while standing next to it (fig. 1-34).

Unfortunately, these fragile figures are an attraction to vandals on motorbikes or off-road vehicles, putting them at the head of the "endangered species" list of rock art types. They are easily damaged or destroyed

1-32 Geoglyph, large human figure near Blythe, California. Geoglyphs here are made in similar ways to those of Chile and Peru.
[This figure has a fence around it which has been only partly successful at preventing damage from vandalism and off-road vehicles]. Photo C. W. Clewlow.

1-33 Geoglyph, the Westbury Horse in England. An example of a chalk figure, in which overlying turf is removed to allow the white lower layer to show through. Photo 1987.

1-34   Geoglyph area, Guatacondo, Chile.   Photo Joan Seibert, 1965.

1-35   Desert area (Borrego, San Diego County, California) cleared of rocks to show underlying sand.   This one is a house-ring, not a geoglyph.   Photo T. Tetherow, 1976.

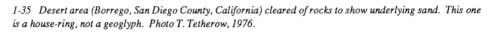

40

by vehicle tracks criss-crossing them (fig. 1-32). Because they are not always readily visible on the ground, some of the destruction is accidental rather than intentional, but the result is the same.

Rock alignments are figures made by moving available rocks or small boulders into various patterns, generally rocks small enough to be picked up and moved by one person. Some of these are linear arrangements, some are circular. The latter have been called medicine wheels, and are most likely related to solstice and celestial observations. Like intaglios, rock alignments are difficult to spot on the ground. Plant growth, wind-blown sand and flash flood debris have buried many ground figures. There is also some possibility for misinterpretation here, since alignments of stone may in fact be house rings, wall remnants, or other features not related to rock art (fig. 1-35).

RELATIONSHIP BETWEEN TECHNIQUE AND STYLE

Each of the methods of manufacturing rock art images calls for slightly different recording methods. The techniques outlined in this manual are primarily applicable to pictographs and petroglyphs. Ground figures are relatively rare and occur in few areas, and their documentation is primarily a job of mapping and/or photography from some elevation.

This discussion of the various techniques of producing rock art indicates the great variety of ways in which prehistoric people chose to create images. Within each of these techniques there is a multitude of artistic styles. The artists did not make random pictures; they followed the customs of their particular culture to create the art. In some regions and time periods, the rock art is almost entirely geometrical and shows almost no recognizable pictorial images of humans or animals (figs. 1-36 to 1-38). In other areas pictorial images are dominant and geometric elements very scarce (figs. 1-39 to 1-41). Styles also changed through time, so that the same area may show several different styles representing different eras of rock art production.

In documenting rock art, the style of the art is more important than

Examples of geometric or abstract rock art. Fig. 1-36 has a zoomorph (deer?), and fig. 1-37 has a recognizeable anthropomorph but the rest of the elements are entirely geometric.

1-36 Polychrome pictographs, Painted Cave, Santa Barbara County, California. Photo 1983.

1-37 Figure combined with primarily geometric pictographs, Rocketdyne Site, Los Angeles County, California. Photo 1979.

1-38 Red and yellow geometric pictographs at Wallabi Gap, Train Hills, Northern Territory, Australia. Photo 1986.

Examples of naturalistic or representational rock art, in which recognizeable pictures of humans and animals are present. The same rock art site may also include geometric elements as well as some forms which are so stylized as to be impossible to identify in detail.

1-39 Mountain sheep, painted in red and black. Flechas Cave, Baja California. Photo 1962.

1-40 Deer, painted in red and black. Gardner Cave, Baja California. Photo 1962.

1-41 Petroglyph of rabbit, Angostura, Baja California. Photo Jack Schwartz, 1977.

the technique. The methods discussed above occur in most areas of the world, but the styles produced by particular groups of people are often distinctive, localized, and easily recognizable. As noted by Schaafsma (1980:8), "A shared repertoire of rock art elements, figure types, figure complexes, and aesthetic modes—hence style—thus signifies participation in a given ideographic system and, in turn, in a given communication network." Therefore, the artistic style provides the basis for recognizing particular culture-historical traditions, assigning them to a time period, and also (hopefully) for developing some interpretation of the meanings of the different sites. An example of a clearly recognizable style is the so-called "X-ray style" of Australia, in which paintings of animals show the internal organs and skeleton (figs. 1-42, 1-43). Production of this style is facilitated by the polychrome painting technique which allows for much detail.

Even a simple petroglyphic rendition of animals can show traditional and distinctive ways of representing the images. Two styles of portraying mountain sheep are seen in figs. 1-44 and 1-45. Although both examples are from the western United States, the styles differ in several details: the mountain sheep from California (fig. 1-44) have plump oval bodies, exaggerated linear horns, and little or no indication of hooves. The Utah examples differ in all these details. The overall style of the two areas includes distinctive ways of representing human and other forms as well. The two styles are widely found in their own areas, showing that the early artists had an established pattern which they followed in producing their petroglyphs.

There is a functional relationship between style and technique. For example, painting allows for fine detail which is not feasible in petroglyphs chipped into a rock surface with a hammerstone. Although the basic style may be easily recognizable, a petroglyph of a mountain sheep, deer, or lizard, for example, will rarely look exactly like a painted picture of the same animal, even if the two images might have been made by the same artist.

The definition of "style areas" or "style periods" is particularly

1-42   Polychrome human figure, Nourlangie Rock, Northern Territory, Australia. Photo 1988.

1-43   Polychrome fish, Northern Territory, Australia. Photo Ron Uzan, 1988.

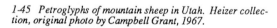

1-44   Petroglyphs of mountain sheep. Little Petroglyph Canyon, California. Photo 1979.

1-45   Petroglyphs of mountain sheep in Utah. Heizer collection, original photo by Campbell Grant, 1967.

Portrayals of rabbits done in the same style; 1-46 is a pictograph; , 1-47 is a petroglyph.
1-46 Tinaja de Refugio Site, central Baja California. Photo by Esther Schwartz, 1976.

1-47 Gardner Cave, Baja California, Photo 1962.

important in some areas where the people apparently made use of more than one technique of rock art at the same time. An example is Baja California, where both petroglyphs and pictographs of fishes, rabbits, and deer were apparently produced by the same people (fig. 1-46, 1-47).

2

PREPARATION FOR RECORDING A ROCK ART SITE

There are two aspects of preparation for documenting a rock art site. The first is the practical aspect of assembling needed materials and supplies. The second is to research the site before recording it. It is assumed that the recorders are outdoor types who have enough sense not to go wandering off into remote areas by themselves, without food or water, and without telling anyone where they are going. Advice on camping out is not necessary for this volume, but many rock art sites are found in areas accessible only on foot, so be certain you have the necessary basic hiking equipment and clothing. Appendix C provides a reminder list of useful equipment for field recording. It is a good aid for field workers who, however experienced, might otherwise manage to forget one or two key items and experience great frustration.

Your first step in preparing to record a rock art site is to find out whether it has been recorded before.

LOCATING SITE RECORDS

If the site is known already, it would be helpful to see what kind of a record already exists so that you can take up where others have left off. There already may be some preliminary notes and even a reasonably good sketch map of the site. There are several places where you can find out whether a rock art site is known to exist at the location you have spotted:

• **Regional summaries and publications on rock art**

• **Museums, Universities, State Historic Preservation Offices**

• **Societies devoted to rock art studies**

REGIONAL RECORDS
AND PUBLICATIONS

Check the regional publications on rock art for your area. Many states, counties, and other regions have general summary volumes on the known rock art of their area. Several of these are listed in the regional summaries in the bibliography. These reports may not be complete and up to date, but they will list the best-known and studied locations. Even if your site never has been recorded, the summary volumes will provide valuable comparative information on nearby sites and will give you some understanding of what is known for the region.

Ordinarily, published reports will not identify the exact location of the sites. Indeed, **it is considered unprofessional, if not unethical, to publish a guide-book to unprotected sites,** because of the threat of vandalism, illicit digging, and other damaging actions to archaeological remains by some visitors. Protected sites (those in parks patrolled by rangers, for example) may well have their locations published and/or marked with signs, although even in these cases you are apt to find directions only to developed tourist attractions, and not to all the rock art sites which are known in the scientific record.

Some published summaries of rock art, particularly the older ones, do give fairly precise location information. But even if maps or directions are not included, you can often recognize the site you are recording from photos or descriptions given in the books you consult.

MUSEUMS,
UNIVERSITIES,
AND STATE OFFICES

Museums or universities with archaeological programs will have site records from their local areas. An archaeologist familiar with the region may be able to tell you whether or not your particular rock art site is recorded in their files. These regional archaeological centers also may have environmental impact reports from contract archaeology projects. These often are unpublished but they may be very detailed. The offices sometimes will let you consult their records or check their maps, but they will want to know who you are and what you are doing before giving you site locations, because of the problem of vandalism. At the University of California, Los Angeles, there is a specialized **Rock Art Archive** (address the Institute of Archaeology, UCLA, Los Angeles, CA 90024) which has records and maps for a very large number of sites in the United States and a considerable amount of information on rock art locations in other countries.

If no local archaeologist is available to provide information, each state has a **State Historic Preservation Office** (usually in the state capitol), which maintains records of all the recorded archaeological sites in the state. A phone call to that office may lead you to information about your site.

ROCK ART
SOCIETIES

There are societies and organizations specifically dedicated to rock art studies. The largest national organization in the United States, the **American Rock Art Research Association** (P.O. Box 65, San Miguel, CA 93451) has members who can provide information on hundreds of sites which they have visited and sometimes recorded. There are similar organizations in Canada, Australia, and other countries. These organizations can provide you with useful information as well as the chance to meet others with the same interests.

WHAT IF
THERE IS
NO RECORD?

These efforts to learn something about your site need not take a tremendous amount of time and effort, but the phone calls and library visit will make your own time in the field more effective. Often you will find there is no formal record of your site; it may be totally unknown, or perhaps only the location has been recorded. Even if there are photographs, notes, and/or a published paper on the site, this does not necessarily mean that there is no further recording to be done. Many older reports include only a couple of photos of the most obvious rock art present—they rarely include *all* of the rock art. Even though recorders may make a conscientious effort to record a site completely, they frequently find when they revisit a site, that they missed some elements. Only a very small handful of sites, even among all of the published sites, have complete and up-to-date documentation, so you can always assume that there is more useful recording to be done. If nothing else, you will be able to record the condition of the site as of the date of your work, and that is invaluable information for future researchers who can compare your record to older records. Aside from the new information you will be able to provide, it will be possible to evaluate weathering and damage over a period of time and gain important insight into the need for preservation of the rock art.

COMPLYING WITH THE LAW

Always obtain permission before entering public or private land for purposes of a recording expedition. Land owners or managers need to know that you are there and doing something constructive, otherwise they will consider you a trespasser, or perhaps worse, a collector or vandal. Archaeological sites on public land are required by law to be protected; sites on private land are often fiercely protected by the property owners, who may take a strong interest in the rock art on their land.

Archaeological sites are protected under a variety of federal, state, and local regulations, and since all rock art locations are part of the archae- ological record, they are included under these antiquities regulations. There is some question about the application of these rules to rock art sites and whether or not it is necessary to get a formal permit to study a rock art site. If one is merely a visiting "tourist" taking notes and photographs, there is nothing to discriminate a rock art recorder from any other visitor to the site. Since no damage is done to the site, it is doubtful whether any- one would choose to raise the issue of a permit. On the other hand, if you have gone to the level of having an "expedition," with several people, mapping equipment, and a tent camp, you unquestionably should clear this operation with the land managers and comply with whatever require- ments they maintain.

To avoid problems with property owners, and to maintain good will toward your own party and all future researchers, it is essential to ad- here faithfully to any agreements or conditions. Pay particular attention to the following points:

• ENTRY: Find out the best way to approach the site and follow the the roads or trails indicated by the property owner. Do not drive across open land unless this is ex- pressly allowed.

• GATES: *Leave gates exactly as you find them.* Close the closed ones; leave open those which were open when you arrived. There is no faster way of antagonizing ranchers and farmers than thoughtlessness about gates and livestock.

• CAMPING: If you are allowed to camp on the property, be extremely careful about using fire and not polluting water sources. Remove all your trash and litter when you are through with your project. You are not allowed to bury cans and trash on public lands; it is a courtesy to follow the same rule on private land and take out all refuse for disposal in a dump.

• NO UNAUTHORIZED DIGGING OR COLLECTING: Many rock art sites are located on or adjacent to archaeological sites with cultural material on or beneath the surface. **Your permission to record the rock art is not permission to do any digging or collecting of artifacts.** The United States and most other countries have antiquities laws which declare archaeological remains (including rock art) to be part of the national heritage and the property of the nation. Should you see archaeological remains associated with the rock art, such as bedrock mortars, arrowheads, shells or bones representing food remains, or stone chipping waste, carefully note the items. They should be drawn or photographed, since they may cast light on the people who made the rock art you are studying. Do not make a collection of artifacts. When they are taken out of context, they cannot be properly studied. If there is a significant amount of cultural material accompanying the rock art, it should be noted in your report and also called to the attention of your State Historical Preservation Office or local university. See ARARA code of ethics (Appendix D).

OBTAINING PERMISSION TO WORK

**RECORDING
ON PRIVATE
LAND**

Allow plenty of time prior to your trip to obtain the necessary permission. The people you need permission from may not be available immediately. It may be necessary to contact others in addition to the property owner, such as a tenant if the land is leased. A preliminary telephone call may speed things up and give you a clear idea of whom you have to contact.

54

Send the property owner a letter stating:

- *what you propose to do*
- *when you would like to be on the property*
- *how many people will be in the party*
- *where copies of your records will be preserved (museum, historical society, etc.)*
- *reassure the property owners that your party will not:*
  leave any litter or trash
  forget to leave gates as you found them
  collect or damage anything

Enclose two copies of your letter and a return envelope. Ask the property owner to endorse one and return it to you if he is willing to grant permission. This will give you written and legal permission to work there, a valuable document which you can show to anyone who questions your right to be on the property or conduct your study. The permission letter is also a formalized acknowledgment of the obligations and agreements which apply to you and your field workers. Be sure to inform anyone who is working with you of the conditions you have agreed to, and remember that *you* signed the letter and it is *your* responsibility to insure that its provisions are met.

To determine who owns private land, the simplest method is to ask the residents or adjacent property owners. If the property has a street address, you can take this directly to the county tax office to track down the owner. If this doesn't work, mark the location to be researched on a USGS (United States Geological Survey) Quadrangle map (the biggest scale you can get, preferably 7.5 minutes) and take this map to the County Tax Assessor's office. The Assessor has books of maps covering the entire county, and the personnel in these offices will help you find the correct parcel map. When you have found the property on the map, note its "parcel number."

To use the parcel number to determine property ownership:

> • *Check the parcel number index in the Assessor's office. The index will give you the name of the owner and a description of the parcel.*
>
> • *Check the Assessor's alphabetical index of the tax rolls. You will find the current address for the owner or the owner's agent and property lessee.*

RECORDING
ON PUBLIC LAND

For public lands, there may be some special permission form that needs to be obtained, but it doesn't hurt to start with the simple letter. It shows that you are business-like and responsible, and if there are any questions or problems, they will come up at this point. If your project is small and of limited duration, even managers of public lands can often grant permission by letter. Discussion with the property managers will also give you information about roads, gates, water, and fires. The manager may know something about the rock art, too, and can sometimes provide information about it, such as who has been there before, and any previous damage to the site.

Much "public" land is, in fact, under considerable restriction or even closed to the public. Public lands might be leased to farmers, loggers, or resort operators, for example. Certain lands are closed to protect endangered species in their natural environment. In the western United States, extensive areas are off-limits during dry periods when the fire hazard is high. You will need to be able to define exactly the area in which you want to work, to determine restrictions on entry. Sometimes the land managers will be able to tell the location from your general description of your rock art site (or may even know of the site), but you may have to identify the area of your work on a detailed map (see discussion of mapping below). Permission to enter closed public lands may be obtained by contacting the nearest office of the following agencies which manage most public land in the United States.

MANAGERS OF FEDERAL LAND IN THE U.S.

- Bureau of Land Management, Department of Interior
- National Forest Service, Department of Agriculture
- National Parks, Department of Interior
- U.S. Army Corps of Engineers, Department of Defense
- Wildlife Service, Department of Interior
- Army, Navy, other users of military reservations

Most of the large areas of public lands are clearly marked on all maps, often even on road maps. For smaller areas such as military posts, state and national parks, or similar units with resident land managers, you can contact the person in charge directly. Most officials are helpful and supportive once they know who you are and the nature of your project. It is to your advantage to promote this relationship even if it involves writing letters and filling out forms. It will save you problems from an administrator who may react to a second-hand report from someone who sees you at work and wants to file an inquiry or complaint. In some of the more remote corners, it is also to your benefit that someone knows where you are and when you will be returning. A minor accident or injury, even a sprained ankle, can be a serious matter if you are a long way from help.

COURTESY
IS THE
BEST POLICY

It is a very important and often-overlooked courtesy to let the property owners know something of what you recorded about the rock art. They are interested in what is on their land, and a letter or report from you after your work is done will not only please them but will perhaps stimulate them to take a special interest in the rock art site and its protection. *If your work leads to some kind of published report, by all means try to get a copy to the property owners.* This is often difficult to remember since it is not uncommon for years to elapse before published reports are available, and in some instances the property will have changed hands. Even so, it is strategic to remember to provide the property owners with a copy of whatever reports, notes, and photographs are likely to be of interest to them. They also like to know where the full manuscript material is deposited. Universities and museums are not infrequently visited by the children and grandchildren of property owners who have passed on family stories of the research that was done on their property.

If you use common sense and courtesy when you are on other people's property, you will assure that future researchers will find cooperative land owners when they want to record sites. The motto of many conservationist groups is a good one to follow: "Take nothing but pictures; leave nothing but footprints."

RESEARCHING THE ARCHAEOLOGY AND ETHNOHISTORY

After reviewing all these cautions and prohibitions, a final suggestion is to read about the aboriginal people who inhabited your area of study in the past. *Rock art is ultimately recorded because of our interest in the artists and their way of life, as well as the art itself.* We would like to know what was in the minds of the people who produced all these enigmatic images. Why is it located where it is? What drew the people to this location rather than other places that look equally likely? What was the motivation for the art? What is the message that was being communicated? The whole recording process is merely to provide the basic data which will lead to answers for questions like these.

To gain insight into what may have been in the minds of the artists, it is essential to have some knowledge of their way of life and their belief systems. Clearly they were influenced by *their* experience and *their* world view, not our contemporary knowledge and perspectives. Fortunately, there exists a large body of literature which can provide some understanding of the way of life of the people who produced the rock art. This is to be found in the ethnographies of tribal peoples who inhabited the study area. The folklore and mythology of these peoples is also a potentially invaluable source of information about what was in their minds, and therefore what was important enough to be symbolized in rock art. There is a great thrill in reading this literature and suddenly gaining an understanding of what certain rock art is likely to mean—a reason for interpretation that is based on the mental set of the artists.

Not all interpretation comes from books. There are still areas of the world where people are making and using rock art today, Australia being the outstanding example. It is worth asking contemporary tribal peoples about the rock art; important information has come from living peoples in Canada, the Southwestern U.S., and Mexico about rock art, its purpose and meanings. Present-day people sometimes have memories of rock art produced by their parents or grandparents, and in addition they may well know myths and stories about the rock art location. Invaluable information can sometimes be obtained if you are working in a region where the native cultures still exist and where there are people who retain knowledge of rock art practices.

Of course, utilizing the literature on native life of recent times may not apply in detail to the art of thousands of years ago. However, general ethnographic features remain for very long periods, and for better or worse, ethnographic analogy is our best source of plausible and convincing explanations for rock art. The task of recording rock art is made much more fascinating and rewarding if the recorder has acquired some basic knowledge of the native peoples, past and present, who produced the images we see preserved on the rocks.

3

BASIC RECORDING:
MAPPING & RECORD FORMS

BASIC RECORDING PROCEDURES

1. Record the site location on a map.
2. Explore the site area to locate all of the art .
3. Record standard observations.
4. Make a sketch map.
5. Fill out a site record form.
6. Photograph the rock art.
7. Draw the rock art elements and motifs.

Each of these recording steps can be carried out on varying levels of complexity depending on the size of the site and the time you have available. Some may require additional techniques as discussed in a following chapter. If you find you can't complete all of the steps listed, take them in order and go as far down the list as you can. Consider each of these procedures as one phase of the research. For a small site, all of these steps may be completed in a day—for a very large site, repeated visits may be required to make a comprehensive record. If you estimate how long it will take you to accomplish each step, you will have some idea of the labor needed and you can set priorities. These steps are the main phases of the recording operation, but there may also be phases within some of these. For example, photographing the site is easy if there are only a few elements present, but if there are 3,000 figures at the site, even the photography will have to be broken down into phases, with the first couple of rolls of film aimed at getting general views and a cross-section of the key elements at the site. A later effort is devoted to thorough documentation of all the drawings including those that are less visible due to weathering or fading. The time needed to make the record can be greatly increased if the rock art is obscured or difficult to see due to vandalism, superimposition of one picture on top of another, exfoliation, or deterioration of the rock surface.

It is possible for a systematic recorder who knows what he is doing to "blitz" a rock art site and get most of the information in a very short time. Some solid published accounts have been based on only a few days of field research at a rock art site. However, the ultimate goal of the researcher is to record 100% of the art and to collect enough data so that the site could be reconstructed if necessary. Whether avocational or professional, the fun of doing it is to assemble the complete record and to make the discoveries that no one else has noticed. The scientific value, of course, is that if the rock art deteriorates, or the site is destroyed in the future, at least there will be a record of the way it once looked, and the artistic efforts of prehistoric peoples will be known and available for further analysis and interpretation whether the site survives or not.

RECORDING SITE LOCATIONS ON A MAP

An essential first step when you find a rock art site is to record its location on a map. Future visitors would like to be able to find the place, and you may want to go back yourself. In some areas, particularly if you are referring to a boulder in the middle of a slope covered with boulders, or to a small cave in a cliff full of small caves, finding the rock art for a later visit may not be easy. Experience shows that it is often very difficult to find rock art locations even from fairly detailed notes made years earlier. Creeks often change their course. Roads, fences, and other landmarks are removed, altered, or concealed by changes in vegetation. Subdivisions, reservoirs, and other construction activity may completely change the appearance of the area.

It is also important to know the exact location in order to separate out new records from those of nearby sites. The records in the UCLA Rock Art Archive include many manuscripts which are detailed in recording the rock art itself, but the location remains a mystery. In some cases, this has led to recording the same site under several different site numbers. In one instance, two quite different-appearing records seem to pertain to the same site, but it is not possible to be sure. There are also several cases where visitors have had great difficulty in finding the sites because their mapped locations were wrong by up to a mile. Hence, while it seems self-evident that there should be an *accurate* map location recorded, a surprising number of records, including some made by professionals who should know better, simply fail to include reliable information on this critical point.

MAPPING OPTIONS

- Notes and a road map or hand-drawn sketch map of area
- Simple triangulation using a U.S.G.S. map
- Universal Transverse Mercator (UTM) system
- Public Land Surveyor System (Sections and Townships)
- Other mapping systems

**ROAD MAP
OR
HAND-DRAWN MAP**

It is very important to explain in your notes how you got to the site, and to mention features or landmarks which helped you find it, including such things as:
> *Public roads or trails*
> *Railroad tracks*

Telephone poles
Streams or dry creek beds
Drawing or photograph of horizon, cliff face, or silhouette
    of rock formations
Springs
Distinctive rock outcrops
Fences, gates
Large trees or other striking vegetation
Other works of man such as buildings or culverts
Best of all, measurement from a benchmark (see below)

If you work with a detailed topographic map, you may be lucky and find a benchmark or permanent surveyor's marker on or near your site which makes it easy to give a precise location (fig. 3-1). Such marked survey monuments are rarely at your site, however, and in locations such as deserts and jungles, it may be difficult to find *any* obvious feature that can serve as a guide to the site. Here, road distances and compass directions may be the only way to relocate a site. Mark the location on a road map if you don't have a topographic map, showing how you reached the rock art site from a road or landmark.

Some field workers have used a technique that is standard for making navigational charts showing the coastline: make a small profile drawing of what the landscape looks like from some point where you can see the site (fig. 3-2). This can be amazingly helpful and can allow ready location of a site from a considerable distance. A good "long shot" photograph of the site area can serve the same purpose. These can be a great aid in finding the site visually, but you still need to know how to get to the place from which your photo or sketch can be of use—hence the need for a map location.

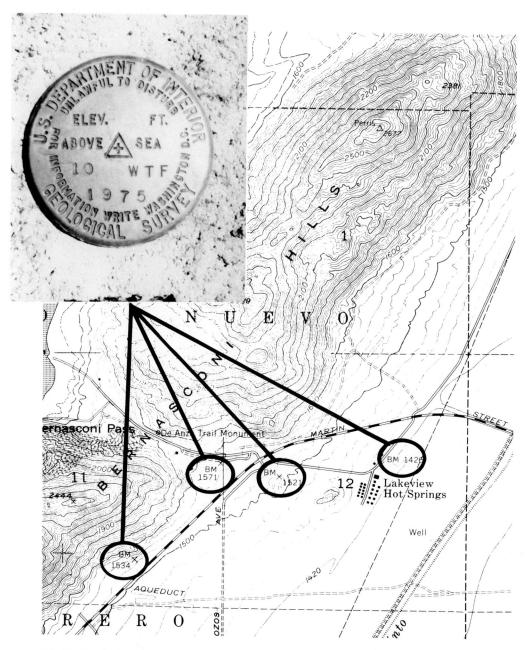

3-1 Portion of a topographic map showing benchmarks. At each of these locations there should be a bronze marker like the illustration in upper left corner. These are usually on the surface, set in a small concrete block or in native rock. They can be obscured by vegetation or slope-wash. Once located, however, you know your exact location and elevation. If you record the distance and direction to your rock art site from any benchmark, this is all the information necessary for future visitors to find the location. Note: other kinds of survey markers may be left by counties or property owners; these should be noted but they are less useful since they won't appear on topographic maps and they may be removed by construction or other land use.

PUKU RANGI ATUA

VIEW OF SITE DRAWN FACING DOWNHILL AND WEST,
BULK OF PUKU BEHIND
5 NOV. 1983

SITE 4 —

3-2 A sketch showing the general appearance of a site area as seen on the ground. Locations of rock art faces are marked. The site area is Puku Rangi Atua, on Easter Island. An enlarged photographic print may also be marked and serve the same purpose, but in many cases the sketch is easier to use because it eliminates extraneous details. A visitor standing where this sketch was drawn would have no difficulty recognizing the site or finding all the rock art faces that have been recorded. Drawing courtesy of Georgia Lee.

SIMPLE TRIANGULATION
WITH A U.S.G.S. MAP

A United States Geological Survey (USGS) topographic map is generally the most accurate way to pinpoint sites in the United States. Maps of similar detail are available for most other countries. In the U.S., maps pertaining to individual states are available at surveyors' supply stores and some map stores. You can locate the map you need from a posted index for the state. State indexes and individual maps are also available by mail from the United States Geographical Survey, P.O. Box 25286, Denver, CO 80225. If you are not familiar with the map symbols used, you might also request the USGS publication titled *Topographic Maps* (this is Government Printing Office Stock Number 024-00102793-3), from either the USGS at the above address or from the Government Printing Office in Washington, D.C.

If you are using a USGS quad map (7.5 minute or 15 minute quadrangle, or any map with similar detailed topography) you can often plot your exact location by simple observation. For example, if your site is at a creek junction or other feature you can recognize on the map, you don't have to do anything but find your location on the map and mark it. Sometimes, however, there is no nearby landmark with which you can identify your site. Then you have to figure out your location by triangulation. To do this, follow the steps below:

   1. Once at your site location, place the map on the ground with its top facing north. Place a compass on the map over the magnetic north indicator and rotate the map underneath until the compass direction matches the magnetic north line on the map (fig. 3-3). Many maps have two arrows—one for true north and one for magnetic or "compass" north. The deviation may be substantial. [Some maps also show grid north (GN), but this is not relevant to your mapping.] Notes, records, and your own maps are assumed to be using magnetic north unless it is specified otherwise.

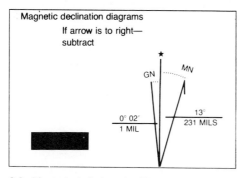
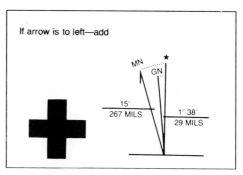

3-3 Magnetic deviation: the difference between true north and magnetic (compass) north. The diagram shows how to correct your compass readings to true north if you wish to do this in your notes. For bearings and azimuths, be sure to note whether your numbers are "true" or "magnetic." The difference in the above examples is 13 and 15 degrees, more than enough to lead to wrong locations on the ground.

   2. Locate a reference point you can recognize on both the map and the terrain such as a creek, mountain peak, lake, reservoir, road crossing, building, or large rock outcrop. The compass direction (bearing) to the selected landmark tells you in what direction the landmark lies, but to figure out where *you* are, you want to know the direction the other way around:

from the observed point to your location. This is a back-azimuth—the reverse direction of your compass bearing. If your compass needle is pointing at the landmark, the back-azimuth will be the direction the other end of the compass needle is pointing (see fig. 3-4). This number of degrees can be read directly from the compass, but it is easier just to figure it by arithmetic. If your compass bearing is less than 180° to the reference point, *add* 180° to get the back-azimuth. If your compass bearing is *more* than 180° to the reference point, *subtract* 180° to get the back-azimuth. Once this angle is known, put a protractor on your landmark (be sure it is oriented in the same way as your map, with the zero point at magnetic north (fig. 3-4). Carefully draw a light pencil line across the map from the reference point toward your direction.   If you have a protractor, the direction line can be precisely drawn. If you are merely using a compass, you can draw the line by eye; this is not precise but will fix your general location.

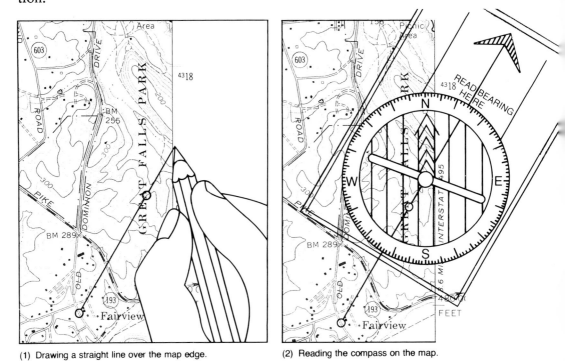

(1) Drawing a straight line over the map edge. (2) Reading the compass on the map.

3-4   Left, a compass bearing from your location (circle next to "Fairview") to a promontory you can recognize on the ground (upper circle). Right view shows map with compass in place to figure the bearing. The back-azimuth is the reverse direction and can be read from compass or protractor (this compass is a simplified diagram and does not show the 360 degrees you would see on your own compass or protractor).

3. Repeat the procedure with two or three other reference points, preferably with points that are about 90° apart.

4. If you have recognized the map points correctly, the lines will intersect. That point is your location. If your lines form a triangle rather than intersecting at a point, you might try to plot a fourth or fifth point. If you still cannot obtain an intersection of three or more lines, check to make certain that each reference point is actually the one you think it is by carefully studying the map. While this is a simple procedure in theory, it can be difficult to impossible if the map is not detailed enough and you are identifying little unmapped hills and gullies on the ground as prominent peaks and canyons on the map. However, in the many cases where there are identifiable landmarks, you will be able to pinpoint your location and precisely mark the site location on the map.

UNIVERSAL TRANSVERSE MERCATOR (UTM) SYSTEM

The national standard in the United States is the UTM system because its metric coordinates are easily computerized and there is no duplication of UTM coordinates; every location on earth has unique referents. The UTM system is widely used by archaeologists and UTM coordinates are required on most archaeological site records. State and national data banks of site information are computerized according to UTM numbers, allowing rapid checking and comparison of site data. Since this is such an important way of identifying site locations, we review the methods for determining the UTM numbers here. For those who might find this an overly complicated subject, pamphlets with detailed information are obtainable from the U.S. Geological Survey Office, Mapping Division, 345 Middle-field Road, Menlo Park, CA 94025.

In the UTM system, the earth is divided into 60 zones running north and south, each covering 6 degrees of longitude. Each zone is numbered (most of the United States is included in zones 10 through 19), beginning at the 180° meridian near the International Date Line. On a map, each zone is flattened and a square grid is superimposed on it. The grid is marked off in meters, and any point in the zone may be referenced by citing its **zone number**, its distance in meters from a referencing line (**easting**), and its distance in meters from the equator (**northing**). These three figures: the zone number, easting, and northing, make up the complete UTM grid reference for any point and distinguish it from any other point on earth. The specific UTM number is determined with a UTM Coordinate Grid (fig. 3-5).

The UTM **zone number** is printed in the legend at the lower left corner of topographic maps, and the full coordinates are given near the northwest and southeast corners of the map, with remaining coordinates shown as blue ticks at 1000-meter intervals along the edges. *Note that the UTM grid system does not match latitude and longitude lines, state plane coordinate lines, or township, range, and section lines on the map.* Since some maps show all of these grid systems, it is important not to confuse one with the other.

The zone number is easy to determine since you merely read it off the map, but determining the exact UTM reference for your site is not easily done in the field and many field workers merely include in their records a xerox copy of that portion of the USGS map on which their site is marked, leaving it to some worker in the office or laboratory to identify the UTM reference numbers. If you want to define the UTM reference yourself, you need the following:

1. A flat work surface on which the map may be spread out.
2. A straightedge long enough to reach across the whole map—generally 30 to 36 inches (ordinary rulers or yardsticks may not be quite straight)
3. A very sharp pencil (don't use ink on the map)
4. A UTM coordinate grid which allows measurements of fine subdivisions of the grid (fig. 3-5). To use this, pencil lines should be drawn across the map to the UTM ticks which are directly west and south of the point you wish to record. The

70

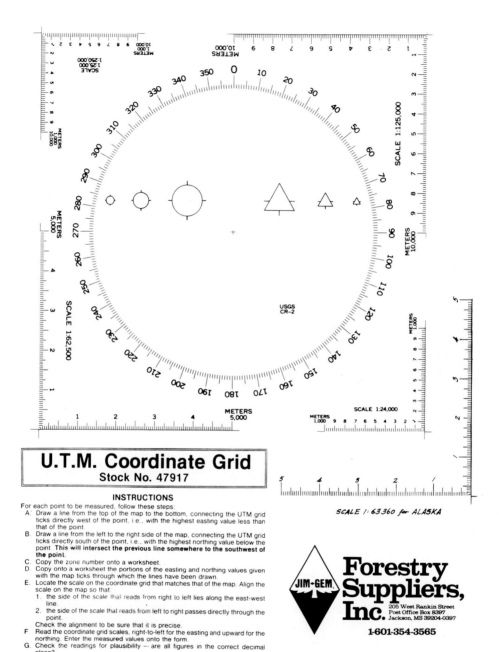

U.T.M. Coordinate Grid
Stock No. 47917

INSTRUCTIONS

For each point to be measured, follow these steps:

A. Draw a line from the top of the map to the bottom, connecting the UTM grid ticks directly west of the point, i.e., with the highest easting value less than that of the point.

B. Draw a line from the left to the right side of the map, connecting the UTM grid ticks directly south of the point, i.e., with the highest northing value below the point. **This will intersect the previous line somewhere to the southwest of the point.**

C. Copy the zone number onto a worksheet.

D. Copy onto a worksheet the portions of the easting and northing values given with the map ticks through which the lines have been drawn.

E. Locate the scale on the coordinate grid that matches that of the map. Align the scale on the map so that:
  1. the side of the scale that reads from right to left lies along the east-west line.
  2. the side of the scale that reads from left to right passes directly through the point.
  Check the alignment to be sure that it is precise.

F. Read the coordinate grid scales, right-to-left for the easting and upward for the northing. Enter the measured values onto the form.

G. Check the readings for plausibility — are all figures in the correct decimal place?

H. Check the figures for accuracy by remeasuring.

I. Be sure that the correct order is observed; zone number, easting, northing (Z,E,N).

SCALE 1: 63360 for ALASKA

Forestry Suppliers, Inc.
JIM-GEM
205 West Rankin Street
Post Office Box 8397
Jackson, MS 39204-0397
1-601-354-3565

*3-5 The UTM Coordinate Grid comes on transparent plastic and is available from many map and field supply houses (this one was obtained by mail from Forestry Suppliers, P.O. Box 8397, Jackson, MS 39204-0397). It is very useful because it has all the instructions for use printed directly on the grid. The grids bear a protractor and several scales for measuring UTM coordinates on maps of different scale. **Note:** this reproduction is printed at a reduced size—copies of it **cannot** be used to determine UTM numbers.*

scale (see fig. 3-5) can then be lined up on the pencil lines and the subdivisions read from it. To record the numbers, start at the bottom left hand corner of the map and "read right up"— that is, read the easting, then the northing. The final numbers must be recorded in the right order: zone number, easting, northing (the memory jogger is **ZEN**).

If the area of the site is less than 10 acres, which will be the case for the vast majority of rock art sites, only one centered UTM reference is needed. If the site is larger than 10 acres, plot 3 or more UTM references at the corners.

PUBLIC LAND SURVEY: SECTIONS AND TOWNSHIPS

The Public Land Survey or Rectangular system provides a simple method of describing a *tract* of land (as opposed to a point on a map.) This uniquely American survey system was enacted by the Continental Congress in 1785. Township, Range, and Section lines as well as section numbers are shown in red on USGS Quad sheets for those states which use the system (30 of the 50 states). Locating your site with these designations gives a legal description of the site and may be helpful in determining ownership of the land, since most tax rolls are organized in this way.

Each state is divided by one or more principal **meridians** running north/south and by **base lines** running east/west. *Range* lines are numbered east and west of the principal meridian; *Township* lines are numbered north and south of the base line. The unit of survey is the Township, which is six miles square and contains 36 sections, each one mile square (640 acres). Fig. 3-6 shows the arrangement of the sections.

In order to record the location of a site with best precision, you will want to locate it within a 10-acre area. Fig. 3-6 indicates the subdivision of sections into quarters (160 acres), and these quarters can be further subdivided into 40 acre plots, then into 10 acre plots. Hence a full description of the 10 acre tract in which your site is located might be given as follows

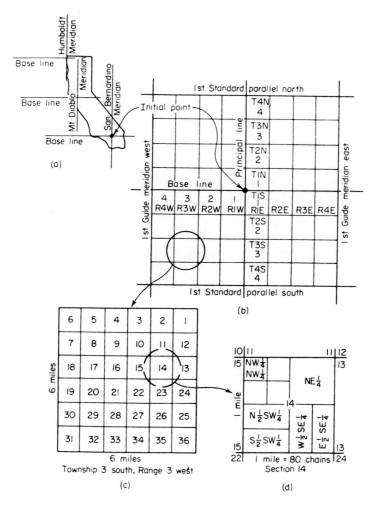

3-6 Locating sites by reference to sections and townships. Townships are numbered from the intersection of a Base Line and a Meridian. Each township contains 36 square miles (sections), numbered as in (c). The individual sections can be further subdivided as in (d) into smaller and smaller units. Reproduced by permission from Civil Engineeering for the Plant Engineer, Robert E. Krieger Publishing Company, Malabar, Florida.

(ordinarily you do not need to record the base line or meridian and can start with the township and range):

San Bernardino	Meridian
T5S R4W	Township and Range Number
Sec. 1	Section Number
SE1/4 of NE 1/4 of NE 1/4	1/4 of the 1/4 of the 1/4

Remember that most USGS maps will have the townships and sections printed on them, so once you have found the square mile in which your site is located the problem is merely to locate which of the smaller units contains the site. To measure the small subdivisions, a very helpful aid is a "40 Acre Land Locater—Type B" available in surveyors' supply stores (fig. 3-7). The locater is a 3.5 by 6.5-inch clear plastic card with marked section subdivisions that can be laid over a section to identify the appropriate quarter/quarter/quarter without drawing lines on the map.

It is desirable to be as precise as possible in recording site locations, but if you are working in the middle of a featureless desert, you may not be able to fix your position as precisely as 10 acres. In such cases, give the location as best you can, but *don't guess* . It is better to be correct about a general location than it is to be wrong about a precise location. Some records in UCLA's Rock Art Archive have very exact locations indicated, but on field investigation they prove to be wrong and therefore confuse the record rather than helping it.

OTHER MAPPING SYSTEMS

Many maps do not show either townships or the UTM grid. Some older maps derived from the military will have a different grid system of numbers. It may be necessary to use these designations if the map does not show the others. Similarly, tourist guides and road maps often have a grid system of their own. These grid systems are too general for precise locations but it is better to use them than nothing at all.

The simplest grids are used on city maps which are often numbered along one edge and lettered along another, allowing you to designate

40 ACRE LAND LOCATER — TYPE B

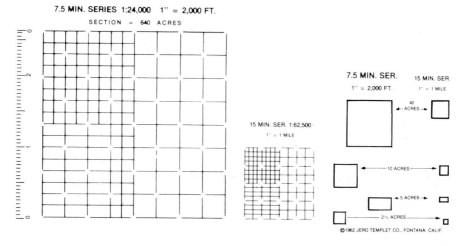

40 ACRE LAND LOCATER TEMPLET — TYPE B

To be used on U.S. Geological Survey Topographic Quadrangle Sectionized or any map drawn to these scales:

2⅝" Section size **7.5 min. series**   1:24,000 or 1" — 2,000 feet
1"   Section size 15 min. **series**   1:62,500 or 1" — mile

Can be used by anyone interested in land by pin-pointing exact location of legally described acreage from 2½ to 640 acres. Guide lines to locate 2½ and 5 acre parcels.

Cut-out squares appearing on right hand side of templet represent the size of parcel from 2½ to 40 acres. When your land is pin-pointed on the map, place the corresponding cut-out square over the area and draw your plot, thus the exact location of your parcel is clearly visible on the map.

Scale appearing on the left hand side is used as a measuring guide to note distance on the ground from the land described to the nearest road or other identifying objects. Distance between each mark represents 100 feet on the land surface.

Jero Templet Co., RIALTO, CALIFORNIA

3-7 Land locater template, used to read subdivisions of sections down to parcel sizes as small as 2 1/2 acres. These come in different scales, on sheets of transparent plastic, to be laid over maps.

a location as "A-5" or some other square within which your location is to be found. This kind of designation is often useful in your own maps of rock art sites and many recorders put their own grid system on their sketch maps to record how the rock art is distributed within the site. The grid may of course be large or small depending on the size of the area—on an individual archaeological site, the grid is usually composed of squares that are only 1 to 10 meters on a side.

Once you have established the location, sketch in the site's approximate boundaries on your printed map. A very small site will be, of course, only a point on a map, but many sites may extend for considerable distances. You should draw a line around the whole area in which rock art is found, and if your map is at a large enough scale it may show details of your site area such as individual rock outcrops, springs, or desert washes. If your map allows you to show not only the location of the site, but how much area it covers, this can be an important part of the record. This is particularly true in the case of sites which may extend for a great distance but are discontinuous, with gaps in the distribution of the rock art.

With the preliminary observations done, you can begin the formal documentation. Two inter-related records are needed: a site record form (examples in Appendix B), and a sketch map (see fig. 4-15). The latter is usually appended to the site record form and is not a formal surveyor's map, but a general layout of the site that is drawn by looking at it.

The primary purpose of the site record form is to document the location and nature of the site. It is not a detailed documentation, but is a key basic report. If this form is filed with the archaeological office of a university, State Historical Preservation Office, or other agency charged with maintaining archaeological site records, it will become a permanent record of the site and will be an important part of the regional records on prehistoric remains. Contact the appropriate office in advance to obtain blank forms for recording sites in the style preferred, or you can copy one of the general forms in Appendix B.

One advantage of filing the site record form is that it will result in a records check to see if the same site is already known. If it is already recorded, you will find what other records exist. If it has not been recorded by anyone, it will be assigned a formal site number which will be the "official" number for the site. These numbers also are integrated into computerized data banks which can be used for rapid information retrieval and for the location of comparative data. *All* formally recorded sites will have a reference number; not all sites will have a name.

If the site is not previously known or designated by anyone else, you are the scientific discoverer of it and you can name it, even though it also has an official site number. The fact that the local bikers' group has their annual picnic there, that the site is marked with graffiti, and that the ground is littered with film boxes and beer cans, shows, of course, that you are not the first person to see the site, but if you are the first person to record the site, you have the discoverer's right to name it. It is a good idea to name your site, because when it is referred to in print, it is far easier to refer to it by a name than by a code number. Nothing is more dull than reading a report full of numbered site designations. If many sites are discussed, the reader has difficulty remembering all the numbers, whereas if the sites are named, it is easier to keep track of them.

Sites are often named after property owners, prominent landmarks, or some feature of the rock art, but you can use any name you wish. Example names of recorded sites include many which are geographic designations (Abka, Sudan; Coso, California; Tamentica, Chile), some which are designations for the property on which they are located (La Española, Costa Rica: name of the ranch where the site is found). Such geographical terms are probably to be preferred since they are not likely to change in the near future. However, some sites are named after their discoverer or property owners, and some have invented names. To be avoided are overly lengthy and complex designations (like "Big Red Rock Amphitheater Site"), names which offer unfounded interpretations of the rock art ("Egyptian Hieroglyph Site," "Shaman's Dream," or "Astronomy Site"), and trite and obvious names that have been used for many other sites such as "Painted Cave" and "Painted Rock." There are dozens of such sites and sometimes two or three in a single county.

WALKING THE SITE TO LOCATE THE ROCK ART

Explore the entire site area to become familiar with it. Try to define the site boundaries. These are often obvious (the walls of a small cave, for example), but the boundaries are not so easy to recognize in more diffuse sites where the rock art may not be in a continuous arrangement. There may be gaps of many yards where no rock art appears. Take the time to sit and look carefully at all rock surfaces for faded panels that might not be noticeable at first. Don't plunge into the recording task until you have familiarized yourself with the art and the way it is produced. Most recorders find that it takes a while to see all the rock art and recognize the elements present. First impressions give only a partial recognition of what is there. The familiarization process may take only half an hour or it may take much longer, but the records will be much better if the recorder has some feel for the whole site and the whole assemblage of rock art that is present.

RECORDING STANDARD OBSERVATIONS

Now comes the time to write down some observations. It should not be necessary to provide this reminder, but those working with other people's field notes are frequently frustrated to find that absolutely essential information has not been recorded. Facts that were obvious and taken for granted by the recorders in the field cannot be known to a later worker who has nothing to go on except written records, and records that cannot be identified lose all value and waste the considerable effort that went into the original work. It is amazing how many detailed documents are filed which overlook the most important fact of all: what it is that the records are recording.

All your notes, records, drawings and photographs require certain basic facts in order to be useful.

ESSENTIAL SITE INFORMATION

- **Name of the site** and its location (include state & country)

- **Recorder's name** (don't use just initials)

- **Date of the record**

The name and location of the site. Many students and some professionals forget to identify what it is they are recording. They spend a great deal of time on records which have no meaning for later workers because they can't identify the name or location of the site. This basic piece of recording seems too obvious to be worth mention, yet many a record has gone into the waste basket because nobody could figure out what the record applied to. The UCLA Rock Art Archive has some site records referring to work done many years ago, for which it is impossible even to identify the *country* in which the site is located. So always include the state or country in the site location.

Your name. Identifying yourself may get you a credit line as a recorder in a publication somewhere, but more importantly it allows future workers to know who did the work. If there are questions or problems, hopefully it will be possible for them to locate you. When several people are working together in the field, since everyone knows the rest of the crew, it is common practice to use just initials rather than the name of the recorder. Unfortunately, when the record is consulted years later, nobody remembers who "J.T." was, so it is better to write out the name.

The date of the record. The inclusion of the date is important because it documents the time the record was made and therefore the condition of the rock art as of that date. Your records may well be examined many years in the future when conditions have changed drastically;

museum and university files often include records that were made over 50 or 100 years ago.

The basic identifiers (site, recorder, and date) are so important that some field workers put them on every page of their records. If you have time during the advance planning for your trip, make up a rubber stamp with this information so you can mark every sheet of paper pertaining to the site (including the backs of photographs). With rubber stamps, it is easy to include the full information and it does not become the burdensome chore it can be when the same data are repeatedly written out by hand. Some exceptionally well organized expeditions have had their own forms and notebooks printed so that every page will have the key information included. The advantage of marking every page is obvious—it preserves the key information even if some pages (or photos) get separated from the rest of the record.

Once your papers have been labeled, you need to write down some standard observations made during the preliminary walk-over of the site area. Aside from the obvious characteristics of the rock art itself, the items that ought to be recorded in your notebook include:

THE GENERAL SETTING

Much rock art was created in spectacular places which appear to have been chosen because of the setting—a natural amphitheater, or a striking cliff or unusual peak. Some locations may have been selected because they are the only available places in the vicinity where rock art could be produced. It is important to describe briefly the features of the natural setting and consider why the site is located where it is. Is there a spring nearby? Is the location associated with trails or passes? Could the site be a "secret place" hidden away from easy view, or is it located to provide a "billboard" to passersby? Is it in the middle of a village or residential location? Is the site in a place with an extensive view of the surrounding country, making it useful for observing game animals or for possible astronomical observations?

THE ARCHAEOLOGICAL ASSOCIATIONS

Rock art may be adjacent to evidences of occupation, such as bedrock mortars, potsherds, darkened soil, faunal remains indicating a midden where people once lived, or chipping waste from stone tool manufacture. Cave sites with rock art often have soot deposits on the ceiling, although these may originate from recent campers. Some rock art sites have no other cultural material in the same place, but many are apt to contain at least some archaeological evidence aside from the art. Such evidences should be noted in the field record. Examples related to rock art include small bedrock mortars or grinding areas where pigment was prepared (sometimes seen with associated cobbles used as pestles), pieces of the ocher or other minerals used for paint, and in dry caves perhaps brushes or twigs used to apply the paint. For petroglyph sites, primarily hammerstones were used to make the grooves; these are rarely found but sometimes occur in the vicinity of rock art.

THE KIND OF ROCK ON WHICH THE ROCK ART IS MADE

If you don't *know* the geological name for the rock involved, collect a little piece of the rock and keep it with your records for later identification by a geologist. This is not done by hammering off a piece of the rock art itself! For some rocks of obvious identification, such as sandstone or granite, this step may not be necessary, but rock art also occurs on several kinds of rock not easy to name. Whether or not you feel it necessary to collect a sample, at the least try to identify the rock.

MAKING A SKETCH MAP OF THE SITE

Although you have already located where the site is to be found on a map of the region, you still will want to make a drawing and/or sketch map of the site area itself, showing the layout of the decorated areas (Figs. 4-15). Sometimes this is a very easy task, but it can be complex and time consuming with rock art that is distributed over many individual rocks or on multiple walls of a cave or rock shelter.

The basic information previously listed as essential for your notes (p. 79) is absolutely essential for maps. In addition, maps require some other data as well. **All** maps, no matter how preliminary and general, lose all utility unless they include such basic information as:

ESSENTIAL MAP INFORMATION
(Without this basic information, the map might as well be thrown away.)

- **Name of the site**
- **North arrow or up arrow**
- **Some sort of size scale**
- **Your name and the date**

Many sketch maps are just that—you stand where you can see all or most of the site and draw a sketch of the arrangement of rocks and rock art. This is useful for a hurried record, but a few simple mapping aids will improve the accuracy and reliability of the sketch map.

THE DATUM POINT

Start by setting up some kind of datum or reference point from which you are going to make all your measurements. The easiest way to do this is to put a wooden stake more or less in the middle of the rock art site, then on a piece of graph paper use a compass and tape measure to plot the distance and direction from this reference point to the various decorated surfaces as they are arranged on the rocks, boulders, and cliffs of the site (fig. 3-8). An alternative for a site which is linear in arrangement (such as a cliff face), is to put a reference line the length of the cliff by using a string and two stakes. The string is pulled tight a foot or so above the ground surface and cannot contact plants, rocks, or other projections which will prevent it from forming a straight line. The string can easily be marked in intervals by using a marking pen every meter, every five feet, or whatever unit is convenient. The features of the site are then put onto graph paper by measuring from the string which provides an axis for the

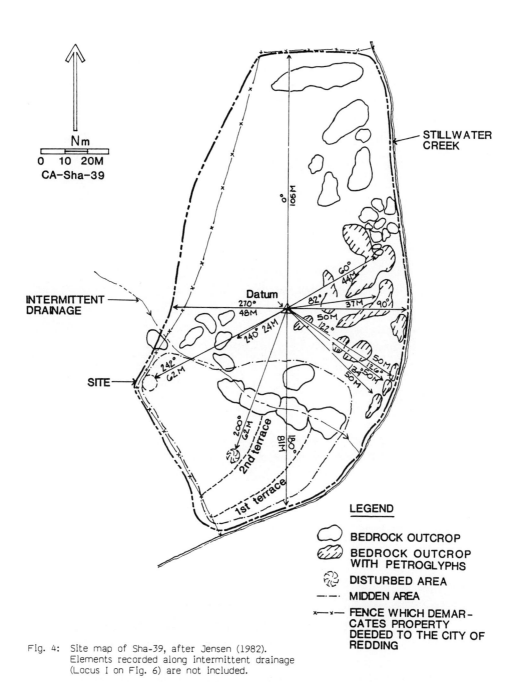

Fig. 4: Site map of Sha-39, after Jensen (1982).
Elements recorded along intermittent drainage
(Locus I on Fig. 6) are not included.

3-8 Sketch map made by measuring in individual rocks from a datum point in the middle of the site. Compass bearings and distances are shown on this map but it is not necessary to include these in the finished sketch map. Reproduced from Van Tilburg, Bock, and Bock, 1987. This map is from a published report which contains details of the location of the site.

site. For very complicated areas, this approach can be expanded by using multiple axes or even staking out a whole grid on the ground to show the relationship of the various parts of the site. At this point, however, you would be making a final map rather than a sketch map, and you might as well do a formal mapping job with a transit. Few recorders will have the equipment or experience to develop such detailed site maps, however. A check list of mapping supplies is provided in Appendix C, but for present purposes we concentrate on the basic gear needed to make a rapid but reasonably useful and reliable sketch map.

THE COMPASS

You need a compass to know which way is north. Make a careful note of which way the rock art is facing, and you may want to note down the deviance between the magnetic north of your compass and true north (this declination in degrees is shown on USGS maps—it changes with time so you need to note the date of the map). Many maps show the annual change in magnetic declination and you can calculate it for the current year. With the discovery that many rock art sites have astronomical significance, the exact orientation of the rock art can be a clue to the meaning of the site. The makers of the rock art did not use a compass, but they often did place rock art in locations from which astronomical observations could be made, and sometimes placed rock art elements in spots which are illuminated by sunrise on the day of solstices.

THE SIZE SCALE

You need some sort of scale or indication of how big an area you are sketching. If the site is small and you have a long tape measure, you can measure directly the major dimensions of the site area. If you don't have a measure, pace off the distances to get some idea of the dimensions. Most people are very poor at guessing distances, particularly if they are looking uphill or downhill, so it is worthwhile to make some effort at measurement rather than just guess at it. One actual site, which was repeatedly documented, stated the size of the site in 9 different places—no two of these observations were in agreement and they varied by over 300% from the largest to the smallest estimate. None of them involved an actual measurement.

A SIGHTING LEVEL:
USEFUL AID
FOR HEIGHT MEASUREMENT

Most sites will not vary much in height, but if necessary, height measurements are easily made with a pocket sighting level available at small cost from hardware and builders' supply stores. These devices allow you to sight along a level line, which is obviously the distance above the ground that your eye is located. Once the bubble is levelled, any point on the ground that you can see is exactly one "height eye" above the level of your feet. By going to that point and standing on it, the process can be repeated up a slope. The total elevation change is simply the number of "height eyes" you have counted. At the top you will have to estimate the last unit, a fractional "height eye", but this method will enable you to make a rapid and quite accurate estimate of elevation changes up to a several hundred feet. Unless your site is spread up a very steep slope, however, it is unnecessary to worry about altitude differences for a sketch map.

FILLING OUT A SITE RECORD FORM

With your sketch map in hand, move to each panel of rock art and write down information about it. These notes are not part of the initial familiarization with the site, but can be done only after you have a sketch map marked with the individual areas of the site. Several standard forms can help in making the drawings and observations, or you can develop your own form so that you are checking things off on a list rather than writing out each observation in detail (See Appendix B). For example, your check list can show the dimensions of each panel, its location, and the direction it faces. Then note some specific observations which will be important to understanding and interpreting the drawings. These are listed below.

THE CONDITION
OF THE ROCK SURFACE

Is it weathering (fig. 3-9), spalling (fig. 3-10, 4-21a), subject to water damage from rain, seeps, or water channels, worn by wind-blown sand? Are there cracks and splits in the rock which may expand to cause the rock art to fall off? Was there or is there vegetation on or adjacent to the rock art (mosses, lichens, plant roots)?

RECENT
(HISTORIC) DAMAGE

This includes direct damage from graffiti (Figs. 3-11, 3-12), spray-paint embellishments (fig. 3-13) bullet marks (fig. 3-14), and efforts to remove the rock art (fig. 3-15a, b). Because most recorders are interested in the ancient rock art, they sometimes ignore all recent graffiti and intrusive elements. Yet these are important for documentation and should not be omitted from the record. In some cases, graffiti and inscriptions have historical importance in their own right. For example, the names of early explorers sometimes appear on a prehistoric rock art site. However, all graffiti including recent vandalism should be recorded. If nothing else, a complete record shows the condition of the site at a particular point in time, and this will be invaluable information for future researchers who can trace the impacts to the site over time.

False or imitation sites also occur. The whole site may turn out to be a recent fabrication, composed of modern art and symbols, sometimes mimicking ancient rock art (Fig. 3-16). Some such locations are close enough copies of ancient rock art to be confusing, but most are readily recognizable as imitations. There is even a copy of elements from the French paleolithic site of Lascaux, reproduced in southern California by a movie company (fig. 3-17). Such locations may have a historic interest of their own and merit a brief record if only to avoid confusions with prehistoric rock art sites.

86

3-9 *Painted deer, arrow shows rear portion removed by natural weathering of the rock surface. Most of the white spots on the body are places where rock inclusions have fallen from the volcanic tuff on which the painting was done. Flechas Cave, Baja California. Photo 1962.*

3-10 *Petroglyph site; arrow shows large surface spall where rock art has fallen off (other spalls are visible on the same rock). The large cracks in the rock have expanded since the rock art was made. Freezing and thawing will eventually break up the rock and destroy the rock art.   McCoy Springs, Riverside County, California. Photo 1978.*

3-11 Damage to rock art from vandalism. The "No Trespassing" sign is painted directly over rock art. Nine Mile Canyon, Utah. Photo 1979.

3-12 Damage to rock art from vandalism. A name and date were put on the petroglyph panel. Sometimes graffiti of this kind may have a value in recording early visits as well as indicating weathering of the surface. In this case, the vandalism was in 1928; the photo was taken 38 years later. Tamentica, Chile.

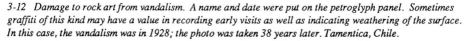

3-13 Damage to rock art from vandalism. A whole site area has been obliterated with spray paint. This can sometimes be removed by trained conservators; in the meanwhile the rock art is effectively destroyed. For this particular site, the paint was successfully removed. Steam Wells, San Bernardino County, California. Photo Frank Bock, 1962.

3-14 A painted rock art figure has lost his left hand to a large spall caused by a bullet impact. Central Baja California, Photo 1962.

3-15a, b Damage to rock art from vandalism. Two pictures of the same panel at Willow Springs, Arizona. Top photo 1976, bottom photo 1977. In the lower picture some of the clan symbols have been removed by chipping off the rock surface. This action is believed to be the result of a conflict among contemporary Indians. These pictures demonstrate the value of having a photographic record taken at different times—repeated photography will document vandalism and weathering through time. Photos Helen Michaelis.

90

3-16 A contemporary rock art site (Topanga, California) produced by a modern painter.
Such imitation rock art and embellishments can sometimes occur with prehistoric rock art. Photo Joan Sei-
bert, 1989.
3-17 A contemporary rock art site (Vasquez Rocks, California), imitating the paintings at Lascaux Cave,
southern France. Photo 1989; the rock art was done some years previously by a movie company to be used in a
film. Many rocks in the immediate area have prehistoric rock art; it is possible that this false site overlies an-
cient rock art because it appears that the whole rock was painted with a background color. Photo 1988.

Finally, the recorder should examine the rock art closely for recent modifications such as re-painting, re-working of petroglyphs, or "additions and embellishments." Such changes may be aboriginal renewal or re-use of the site, but they can also represent tinkering by recent visitors believing they can enhance or "improve" on the work done by the ancient artists who created the site. It is often difficult to decide the true explanation for modified rock art elements, but it is important to recognize and note modifications when they are present.

INDIRECT EFFECTS
WHICH MAY ENDANGER
THE ROCK ART

The most obvious of these is the building of a new road which makes a formerly inaccessible rock art site easy to reach and therefore increases the number of visitors. Other effects that may change the site include deforestation, leading to increased alluviation and run-off, and changing the water courses that may bury the site under slope-wash or even submerge it in a reservoir. Observation of what is happening in the vicinity of the site is therefore important, and may in fact trigger some intense effort at recording and/or preserving the site.

EVIDENCE FOR SEQUENCE
OR CHANGES
THROUGH TIME

It is easy to assume that all rock art found in the same place was made at the same time, but common sense tells us that large rock art sites were not created in a single day. Often they were used for generations or centuries. Some effort needs to be made, therefore, to recognize which elements are older and which are newer, and to note all such evidences.

The most common evidence for periods of rock art production is that of superimposition—an element or drawing which occurs on top of another drawing and therefore must have been created later in time (figs.

*3-18   Painted figures of birds overlie human and animal figures, marking the birds as the most recent paint-
ings of this panel. In this site, repeated over-painting has produced some areas in which there are five layers of
painting. At least four layers are present in this photo, but they are not always discernable from photographs
and require very careful field observation to identify and record. Flechas Cave, Baja California, photo 1962.*

*3-19   Petroglyphs of human figures are overlain by large mountain sheep figures. Superimpositions are direct
evidence for the sequence of art; where there are many of them, they can be used to identify style periods in the
art of a given site or area. Coso, California. Photo 1988.*

3-18, 3-19). In some sites, there are multiple layers of painting represent-ing different episodes of use. You will not know, of course, how much later the upper drawings were made. It might have been one day later or perhaps a thousand years. However, systematic and careful recording of a large number of superimpositions will often allow determination of style periods and can sometimes give clues as to the amount of time involved

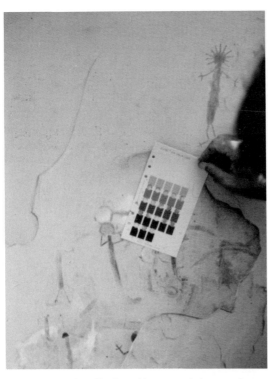

(see discussion of dating). Su-perimpositions are not always obvious and may not have been deliberate attempts to put one figure on top of another. Some-times only a tiny part of one line overlies the earlier rock art. Therefore, it is necessary to look consciously for superimpo-sitions and to record them care-fully. Some sites have no super-impositions, while others are full of them. In complex loca-tions there may be as many as five or six layers of superim-posed paintings (fig. 3-18). Superimpositions often cannot be recognized and sequenced from drawings or photographs, and they cannot be recorded ex-cept by a careful observer at the site—hence notes are essential.

3-20   Use of Munsell color guide to record pigment colors at a pictograph site. Munsell colors afford an accurate color designation and may be helpful in identifying the particular pigments used in making rock art.

Another way of esti-mating sequence is by observing patination of the rocks. Some petro-glyphs appear very light in color when first produced, and gradually darken to match the natural rock surface on which they were chipped. To objectify such observations, it is a good idea to record the actual color of the rock art elements, using the *Munsell Soil Color Chart*   (fig. 3-20) for comparisons. This chart is a book of earth-toned color chips that are numbered for easy reference. Because of the care needed to be sure that every chart has exactly the same color shades, these books are expensive, but they are invaluable for standardized designations of color. The book may be purchased from Munsell Color, 2441 North Calvert St., Baltimore, MD 27218.

Two or more periods of rock art production may be obvious at a site. But many factors affect the rate of patination and color change, so this method of defining time periods requires some careful evaluation and is not reliable for only a few random drawings at the site. However, if there are many elements, and all of a particular subject or style are of one color, and all of another kind of drawing are of a darker color, there is certainly a sequence of rock art production that can be suggested.

Note that determination of *sequence* is not a determination of *age*. You will not know how old the rock art is, nor the amount of elapsed time between the periods of use. Nevertheless, the sequence is important to note. The sequence of styles is particularly important in a regional study, since it allows recognition of earlier versus later sites. Furthermore, once the age of a style is known in one location (from radiocarbon or other dating evidence), that age may be applied to the style wherever it is found. So even if studies of sequence and superimposition do not yield immediate "years ago" ages. they are a first step at sorting out time periods and building a chronology of rock art.

4

BASIC RECORDING:
PHOTOGRAPHS & DRAWINGS

PHOTOGRAPHING THE ROCK ART SITE

Photography can be the single best technique for recording rock art because it is done rapidly and provides an accurate record that is not dependent on how the individual eye sees images. As they say, the camera doesn't lie. If time is limited, it is possible to make dozens of photographs in just a couple of hours, and these can document complex rock art panels that would take hours to draw. Most recorders will find the photography faster and easier than the drawings, and they may want to do the photographic record before tackling the drawings. However, a photograph may not be very useful in later studies unless some attention is paid to taking good pictures with the right perspective, **and the necessary markers are in the photograph** (fig. 4-1).

This manual cannot teach basic photography; it is assumed that the recorder has a camera and some idea of how to make it work. For those completely inexperienced, a few suggestions about equipment and technique are made, and beyond that, the reader is referred to the many books about photography in any library. Introductory photographic manuals are readily available from Eastman Kodak, and for those wanting to develop real expertise, there is a vast amount of highly technical information available. A number of references discuss photographing rock art, including DeKorne (1973), Green (1976), and Hyder and Oliver (1983).

4-1 Example of marker in picture to show site designation, size scale, and which way is up. For rock art on a horizontal surface, the arrow should point north. These markers may not be desirable in pictures intended for published illustrations, so they can be placed at the edge of the picture where they can be cut off if desired. Some recorders prefer to take two photographs, one with the marker and one without. Photo 1990.

Photographs will generally give the best visual impression of the rock art unless the recorder is very skilled as an artist. The photos also serve as a check on the drawings. It is sometimes possible for an experienced person to see things in the photograph that were not seen by the recorder who made drawings. It is also true that some rock art elements have been drawn in quite different ways by different observers (fig. 4-2). A good photo would help to check the reliability of the observer's eye. A photograph can also be very useful in recording deterioration or destruction of rock art when compared with earlier photographs of the same site (figs. 4-3a, b).

Photographs also provide a good view of the setting and the site (see comment on "establishing shots" below). There is one California case in which there are two documents with vastly different representations of the rock art at a site, but there is enough general similarity of the overall record to believe that both of these records pertain to the same site. We can't be sure because the mapping information is also uncertain. In this case, a couple of photographs would resolve the issue immediately, both as to identification of the site and as to which of the two records is

more likely to be reliable.

PHOTOGRAPHIC EQUIPMENT

The Camera. As a preliminary comment, it is better to
use a camera you are familiar with than to insist on
having the most expensive
and complex camera money

4-2 Three drawings of the same petroglyph by different recorders at the site of Marlissa, Guyana. The original drawings were made in 1873, 1976, and 1978. A good photograph would resolve the ambiguities in these reproductions. After Dubelaar, 1981.

can buy. If you are buying or borrowing a camera with advanced capabilities, you should shoot at least a few rolls of film with it before taking it
into the field to document rock art sites. Don't take untried equipment to
the field. You don't want to be on your field expedition when you discover
your camera doesn't work (or you don't know how to work it). Recently
developed cameras include some very sophisticated "point and shoot"
cameras which automatically focus and adjust the exposure (and even fire
a flash if necessary). These greatly improve the odds of getting good pictures by inexperienced photographers who have not figured out all the
camera adjustments and settings.

The standard and preferred photographic tool for recording rock art
is a 35mm single lens reflex camera with interchangeable lenses or a zoom
lens and a synchronized flash unit. These cameras take quality photos and
are ideal for hiking because they are light weight. However, it is possible
to get useful pictures with almost any camera at most open-air rock art
sites. The rocks are not going to go anywhere while you photograph them,
so you don't need either lenses or shutters designed for photographing race
cars or speeding bullets.

Because of lighting problems, photos in caves and rock shelters
may require more costly and versatile cameras or use of very fast film.
You may also use more highly specialized gear if it available (Hasselblad,
Speed Graphics, and large-format studio cameras). One site in California

4-3 a, b   Value of a photographic record taken over a period of time. *4-3a shows a rock art site in the Carrizo Plain, California, taken by Von Petersdorf in 1895. (Photo courtesy Georgia Lee). 4-3b (below) is a photo of the same panel taken in 1980, showing disappearance of most of the very elaborate rock art that was originally present. Arrow points to the same element in both photographs.*

was photographed with an 8 by 10 inch Polaroid camera worth thousands of dollars. The resulting photos are of archival quality and have faithful color reproduction, but nearly equivalent results can be obtained with a 35 mm. camera in the hands of a knowledgeable photographer.

If you want negatives of maximum quality, you may want to induce an experienced photographer to accompany your field trip and take on the responsibility for the photographic record. Some photographers are drawn to the challenge of photographing difficult subjects, and rock art is often difficult to photograph, particularly if it is faded or has little color contrast with the native rock.

Polaroid cameras, even the cheapest of them, may produce good record pictures of rock art. The better Polaroid cameras have larger print sizes and sharper lenses (see discussion of film, below). The instant prints from Polaroid cameras also provide a good check of lighting conditions and reassurance that you have the picture. Nothing is more disheartening than to take film in for processing only to find that the photos did not come out for some reason (see Bock's Laws, appendix E, for a humorous view of photographic mishaps in the field).

Color Film. Color film is a must if you are photographing pictographs, particularly if they are painted in several colors. You can use slide film, which gives you a positive image (ready to project or view), or negative film, which gives you a color negative (from which either slides or prints can be made). **Kodacolor** is an example of a color negative film, **Kodachrome** is an example of a slide film. Most rock art is documented with color slide film which is easy to view and store. Slides also can be projected on top of drawings to check for accuracy.

Some photographers prefer to use color negative film, particularly Kodacolor with a film speed of 100 or 200, because it is possible to make slides, color prints, or black-and-white prints from a color negative. Hence, you don't need more than one camera with one type of film to obtain all the photographic records you want. However, black-and-white prints made from color negatives rarely have the quality you can get from using black-and-white film in the first place. Time and facilities permitting, it is useful to take rock art photos with both black-and-white and color film, the former being used to prepare prints intended for publication. Due to cost, much published rock art is still illustrated with black-and-white photographs; extensive use of color is highly desirable but it greatly increases the cost.

It is important to use a film that you like and that gives you consistent results. Avoid using several different kinds of film and shuffling around from one to the other unless you know what you are doing. It's easy to forget to change the meter settings when switching between films of different film speeds, causing a roll of film to be either under-exposed or over-exposed.

Of the slide films, Kodachrome 25 and Kodachrome 64 give good color saturation in normal light and can handle most rock art recording. They are fairly slow films (the numbers refer to film speed; the smaller the number the slower the speed), but can be easily used in shaded or low-light situations with the help of a tripod and long exposure time, or by using a flash unit. As mentioned above, the rock art won't move, so if you need a 20-second time exposure, why not? Remember, however, that exposures longer than about a second may not be correctly exposed according to your light meter reading. Time exposures require more light than the meter shows, and may also need color correction filters.

It is more reliable to use a flash or a fast film to get an image in low light levels. Kodachrome 200 is a fast film that works well (it can be used with a film speed of 400 but tell your film processor that it was taken at that speed). Both Kodak and Fuji have films with speed of 400 and 1,000— very fast films which can take an acceptable picture even in shaded corners without additional lighting. Kodachrome lasts longer in storage and has better color permanence than Ektachrome. Color negative films (Kodacolor) may be even more likely to last since they will not be projected directly and will be used only to produce slides and prints.

Black-and-White Film.   Kodak Plus X is a standard 35mm. black-and-white film useable in most situations, but the newer Kodak films (TMAX 100 and 400) are better for standard use. If you take both films to the field, the 100-speed is good for sunny areas and the 400-speed is ordinarily fast enough for shaded areas such as rock shelters. Kodak also makes an exceptionally fine-grained film: Technical Pan, with a film speed of only 25. It is outstanding but requires special processing and beginners will probably get better results with TMAX. Polaroid black-and-white film is available with a very high film speed of as much as 2,000 or even 4,000. On the larger cameras it is possible to get Polaroid film that provides both a print and a fine-grain negative with each exposure (this film has a speed of 100). The negatives are of excellent quality, but they must be treated with a chemical solution which may be awkward and messy in field situations, requiring water and containers to mix the solutions. It is also unsatisfactory under many field conditions because it is difficult to keep the wet negatives free of dust while waiting for them to dry. If you use this film, you need to have a cardboard box or some similar container to cover the negatives while they are drying.

Since you can get both black-and-white prints and also color prints from color negative film, recorders may wonder why they should bother to use black-and-white film at all? Aside from publication considerations, discussed above, black-and-white film may take better pictures under some conditions. Many rocks with petroglyphs have only two color tones (essentially dark and light) and don't require color film. A lot of pictograph sites are painted in only one color (usually red or black), and these can also be effectively photographed on black-and-white film.

In addition, you can greatly enhance the contrast of faint rock art designs by using filters with black-and-white film, sometimes to the extent of making the rock art far more visible than it is to the eye or on color film (figs. 4-4a, b). Infrared film, obtainable in both black-and-white and false-color varieties, also can be effective at enhancing the contrast and making the images more visible. Both the use of filters and the use of infra-red film are described in many articles, but it is usually necessary to experi-

4-4a, b   Photographic enhancement of rock art by use of filters.
*4-4a shows granite boulder photographed on orthochromatic film without a filter—the red-painted pictographs
are invisible.*
*4-4b shows the same rock photographed with a blue filter, with rock art clearly visible. [Note: the rock art is
visible to the eye, and photographs well on color film, so this example is an extreme case which rarely occurs.
Invisible rock art is not likely to be made visible by photographic techniques except in very unusual circum-
stances] Site Riv-114, Riverside County, California. Photos 1986.*

ment with these techniques. The right approach for one site does not often work well in another site because of varying conditions of lighting, color of rock, paints used in making the rock art, and other variables. And since you cannot see the effects of special films like infrared until the film is processed, it will take some test rolls of film to discover whether you are getting better pictures.

Lenses. Most 35 mm. cameras come equipped with a standard 50 mm. lens. It is sometimes helpful to have a telephoto lens for taking detailed pictures of rock art high on a cliff or in any location not easily approachable. Lenses with a focal length between 100 and 250 mm. are ordinarily adequate. More important is a wide angle lens (between 20 and 35 mm. focal length) which will allow you to photograph rock art from a short distance. This is essential in tight places where you cannot stand back far enough to get all of the subject into the picture. The ultimate convenience is a zoom lens which will give you many focal lengths. Some of these lenses range from 28-250 mm. in focal length, so that one lens will do everything. A few of these also have a macro setting allowing you to take close-ups of very small elements, from a distance of only a few inches. Photographic purists believe that zoom lenses are not as sharp as individual lenses, but for recording purposes you won't be able to tell the difference. Few recorders have the money, or the desire, to lug a suitcase full of lenses into the field. Most recorders of rock art are happier with one zoom lens that will take all the pictures.

Filters. Filters can be used to correct some lighting problems. Obviously, there are limits to using colored filters with color film, since the pictures will simply take on the color of the filter. Some filters work well with both black-and-white and color films. For example, a polarizing filter will cut down on glare (for all kinds of film) and will improve the color intensity of color films. There are also neutral density filters which have no effect except to reduce the amount of light reaching the film. If you have fast film in your camera (for the shaded areas), the brightness of the light may be too great for photographing in sunny places. Use of a neutral density filter will allow you to take pictures of the bright areas without changing your film. Many other tinted color correction filters are available, but they are primarily for the experienced photographer. The only other filter ordinarily useful with color film is a Wratten 81A filter which will help reduce a blue cast caused by heavy shade.

When using black-and-white film, many colored filters are available which can enhance the contrast between the rock art and the background color of the rock. These filters, which are red, yellow, green, or blue, can sometimes make a dramatic difference in the visibility of rock art elements. You can get a good idea of their effect by looking at the rock art through the colored filter. If you can see an improvement in the contrast, it will show up on the film.

With or without filters, it is worth mentioning that there is a great deal of rock art that looks better in a photograph than it does in the site, because you can improve the contrast by lighting, filters, and exposure times.

Tripod. Adequate documentation is certainly possible without a tripod, particularly if fast film is used. However, the use of a tripod will improve the quality of rock art photographs because it allows you to use the smallest lens aperture (f/16 or f/22) to photograph the art, and using these small lens openings requires slow shutter speeds, often too slow to allow hand-holding the camera without movement.

The smaller lens openings (f/11, f/16, and f/22) will increase your depth of field, thereby insuring that more of your photograph is in focus. This is especially necessary in photographing rock art because elements often occur on uneven or sloping surfaces, so that the camera cannot be placed exactly parallel to the rock art being photographed. Some parts of the rock art will be much closer to the camera than others, which may cause some part of it to be in focus and the rest out of focus. The smaller apertures also increase color saturation and overall picture quality.

When setting up your tripod, try to get the film plane (your camera back) parallel to the panel surface. If it is tilted, perspective distortions

will occur and elements of the image closer to the camera will appear proportionally larger than elements more distant from the camera.

Lighting.   Once you have photographed the general setting of the rock art, take some time to plan your photography of the individual elements based on lighting conditions. Nothing is more important for insuring a good picture than the lighting of the subject. Photographers who learn to see the lighting conditions and know the effect they will produce on film, have little difficulty getting photographs with both documentary and aesthetic value.

Rock art does not usually photograph well in direct sunlight and never when it is in partial light and partial shadow. Cloudy or overcast days are often ideal for photographing rock art because there is even light and no shadows. Color film gives particularly good results with even and diffused light. If it is too dark, of course, you may not have enough light for good color reproduction. If the day is a sunny one, it is important to look at how the shadows are changing.   Film cannot record all the contrast that your eye can see, and part of the picture will be too dark or too light if it is partly in the sun and partly in the shade, even though your eye could see the detail in all parts of the scene. **On most sites, all that is necessary to get proper lighting conditions is to wait until the sun is in the right position.** Often this will prove to be when the sun is very low on the horizon (sunrise is frequently the best because of less wind and dust).

If you are rushed and need photographs of half-lit rock art elements, you can control the lighting by shading the whole area of the photograph with a tarpaulin, blanket, or piece of cardboard such as a flattened box. (fig. 4-5). If the area of the picture is small enough, you can sometimes have a fellow crew member stand in the right place to cast a shadow on the rock art. Small umbrellas also can be carried which can provide shade for both rock art and photographer. These can be combined with the functions of reflectors and diffusion screens if the umbrella is made of the right material (photography supply houses stock several sizes of such umbrellas). A large piece of very lightweight, white nylon is ideal for shading since it will let diffuse, shadow-free light through onto the subject area. This is the same effect one gets on a day of light overcast. Note that if you use a colored object for shade or diffused light, such as a red blanket, it can add a color tone to the picture, so white materials are best.

4-5 Improving the photograph by holding a piece of cardboard to shade the rock art, so that it is not partially in the sunlight and partially in the shade. Most films cannot handle the contrast between shadow and bright sunlight. Without reducing the contrast , parts of the picture will be overexposed. Exeter Rocky Hill, Tulare County, California. Photo 1982.

Reflectors.   An excellent way to increase the light in dark areas (inside caves and shelters, for example) is to make a reflector and use it to direct sunlight to the darker section (fig. 4-6). A simple reflector is made by wrapping aluminum foil around a piece of cardboard. For very small areas a page-size piece of cardboard will do, but a larger reflector made from the side of a cardboard box is better. A beam of light can be reflected on the foil from a great distance to provide enough light for photography even in areas that are so dark that the rock art can't be seen with the naked eye. With multiple reflectors, it is possible to bounce light around corners. Aluminum foil is the cheapest and most effective reflector, but

108

any large white object, such as a sheet, will bounce a lot of light into a dark area.

FLASH PHOTOGRAPHY

If existing light is insufficient to expose your picture, you may need a photoflash unit. A flash may also be used for eliminating harsh shadows that contrast with the daylight. Note, however, that placement of the light source will affect the shadows in the picture and hence the appearance of the rock art. A good rule is to aim the flash at a 45-degree angle to the rock art, al-

4-6 Increasing the light by use of a reflector (in this case a piece of aluminum foil over a piece of cardboard). Riverside County, California. Photo 1981.

though faint paintings are often enhanced if the flash is aimed straight on. It may be desirable to use an extension which allows you to hold the flash away from the camera, rather than immediately adjacent to the lens.

Different flash units will yield differing angles of coverage and differing color fidelity. You should experiment with yours to know how it lights the area and also how it changes the color balance of the film you use. A common problem occurs when you use a wide angle lens with a normal flash, causing you to lose the edges of the picture. Some flash units can be adjusted to vary the angle of coverage, and others can be fitted with an attachment to give the desired coverage. Because of the instantaneous flash of light, you cannot visually see what the picture will look like when it is developed. Most flash photographs are taken at 1/60 second or slower because the shutter can cut off illumination to some part of the frame at faster speeds. Whatever flash unit you use will come with a rating number and instructions for calculating the proper f/stop; you may want to bracket your exposure by using other f/stops as well and taking several pictures of your subject.

Use of flash can often improve pictures taken in daylight; it is not necessary for the subject to be in dark areas. Rocks with irregular surfaces, cracks or crevices, will often have a pattern of shadows on the rock which may partially obscure the rock art, or be obtrusive in a photograph. A flash picture will eliminate most of these shadows and often yield a better picture. With pictographs, flash pictures taken during the day sometimes yield excellent pictures with better color rendition than use of the natural light. This is because the flash has a "pure" color temperature which records colors slightly differently than daylight, with its many reflected colors from the surroundings (rocks, vegetation, etc.). However, since you cannot see what the results of a flash picture will be when you are taking the picture, recorders of rock art find that flash units often do not give as good a result as daylight. Because of the static nature of the subject matter, photographers are able, instead, to use long film exposures or to provide additional lighting by bounced light from reflectors. It is worth experimenting, however, with flash pictures taken in daylight.

NIGHT PHOTOGRAPHY

A good possibility for controlling the lighting to get shadows and other effects is photographing sites at night (fig. 4-7). In the absence of extraneous light at night, photographers can direct the shadows where they want them, using flash or other artificial light to enhance the contrast of the picture. This is particularly effective with petroglyphs since the pecked grooves can be filled with shadows by using side-lighting. On occasion, night photography will also yield more faithful color results since there is no bounce light from the surroundings (rock faces, trees, soil) to reflect different colors onto the rock art. It must be remembered, however, that the people who made the rock art never saw it this way, and little is gained by obtaining the most faithful laboratory type of color rendition, as opposed to the way the rock art looked to the people who made it.

110

4-7 *Control of light by photographing rock art at night. This allows control of the color balance of the light, for accurate color rendition, and also allows the photographer to create the shadows which will enhance the contrast of petroglyphs that may not photograph well (or be clearly visible) in flat light. Hunter Liggett Military Reservation, Monterey County, California. Photo 1981.*

MAKING THE PHOTOGRAPHIC RECORD

The following suggestions for photo documentation of sites have been supplied by a number of experienced and successful photographers of rock art. These are only guidelines, however, because each site presents its own set of challenges. You may need to experiment on your own, and if you keep a careful record of your photographic attempts, you will be able to discover the most effective techniques for each situation.

Establishing Shots. Begin by photographing the overall site and setting. A few of these pictures (called "establishing shots" or "long shots" by photographers) will provide general views of the site and will be invaluable aids for others seeking to find the location, since these general views will show prominent landmarks, outcrops, and other features of the site (fig. 4-8). Sometimes an enlargement of such a picture is better than a sketch map, since the photo can be marked to show all of the principal areas of rock art, such as individual rocks, cave walls, and panels.   These

4-8 Ravine containing rock art (arrow). Site areas may not be visible on the ground from any distance, but a photograph taken from a distance may be a considerable aid to future visitors trying to find the site, since they can use features of the landscape as a guide. Coso, Little Petroglyph Canyon, California. Photo 1986.

general views also give a good idea of thc dimensions of the site and will show site vegetation, geology and general environmental conditions. This is especially informative to future workers and can be very helpful to you in completing your notes if you need someone to identify the plants or geology. There is a standard procedure of taking a long shot (LS), medium shot (MS) and closeup (CU) of the site (Figs. 4-9a, b, c; 4-10a, b, c). This may also be useful for individual rocks, panels, or art elements. Photos taken at different distances supplement one another and give a viewer the feeling of getting closer and closer to the site and its rock art.

A special kind of long shot, important for large sites or panels, is the panoramic view in which the picture is composed of multiple photographs taken along a base line and later assembled into a composite picture. For large sites or areas of rock art, pictures taken from a single

4-9a, b, c   Progressively closer views of the same site as 4-8. In a report on the site, such pictures aid the reader in understanding the context and setting of the rock art. Photos 1986.

4-9a   General view of the ravine containing thousands of petroglyphs on basalt rocks. Person in upper right gives size scale.

4-9b   Closer view of ravine. Again, having a person in the picture gives a size scale. It would otherwise he very difficult for a reader to visualize how large an area is in the photo.

4-9c   Example of the rock art at this site.

4-10a, b, c Another set of progressively closer views for establishing the setting of a site. Painted Rock, Carrizo Plain, California. Photos 1980.

4-10a   View of the large cleft rock outcrop (rock art is in the central enclosure of the rock).

4-10b   Inner part of the rock outcrop.

4-10c   A panel of rock art showing exfoliation and vandalism.

114

position will have serious problems of perspective if it is desired to combine several views into a single picture. Some planning is needed to take multiple pictures and assemble them into a montage. If you want to use this kind of picture, see Saenz, Joyner, and Morrow, *in press*.

Bracketing The Exposure. One of the virtues of 35 mm. film is that it is relatively inexpensive. It is therefore possible to take several pictures of the same subject, changing the exposures (f/stop and/or shutter speed), to be sure that at least one of the pictures has the desired exposure. To bracket, take one photo according to your camera meter reading, then change your camera settings to take one photo with greater exposure and one with less exposure. For example, if your meter indicates the correct exposure to be at f/16, take another picture at f/11 (twice as much light) and one at f/22 (half as much light).

Identifiers In The Photograph. Your photographs will only be useful for future scholars if you pop a few identifiers into at least some of the pictures on each roll of film (figs. 4-1, 4-11). Nothing is more frustrating than the arrival of a big batch of slides or photographs which leave you scratching your head, trying to figure out where that picture was taken and which way is up (figs. 4-12, 4-13, 4-14). Most of what you need to know about the subject of a photo can be placed in the picture and should not require consultation with notes and written records. A good practice is to make the first photograph of each roll a picture of the identifiers—this will give key data for all the pictures on the roll and will "catalog" the negatives provided they are not cut apart.

This critical information can of course be provided in a catalog or notes accompanying your photos, but it is far easier, and less subject to error, to have the data appear directly in the photograph. It also insures that the key information will not be separated from the photo.

The following identifiers can be put in one corner or edge of the photograph (not on top of the rock art):

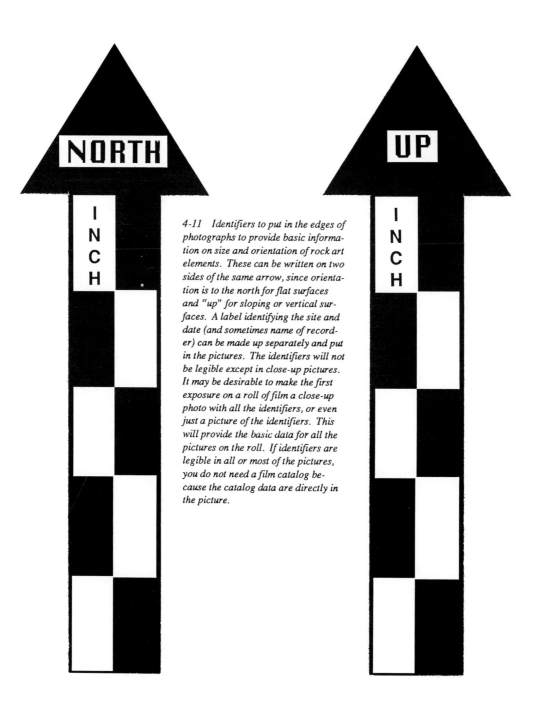

4-11 Identifiers to put in the edges of photographs to provide basic information on size and orientation of rock art elements. These can be written on two sides of the same arrow, since orientation is to the north for flat surfaces and "up" for sloping or vertical surfaces. A label identifying the site and date (and sometimes name of recorder) can be made up separately and put in the pictures. The identifiers will not be legible except in close-up pictures. It may be desirable to make the first exposure on a roll of film a close-up photo with all the identifiers, or even just a picture of the identifiers. This will provide the basic data for all the pictures on the roll. If identifiers are legible in all or most of the pictures, you do not need a film catalog because the catalog data are directly in the picture.

116

**4-12 to 4-14 WHICH WAY IS
UP? Three examples of rock art
photographs which do not have
anything in the picture to tell the
viewer how the picture should be
oriented. An "up" indicator
should be placed in the picture or
photos and slides must be labeled
which way is up.**

*4-12 The diverse orientations of the
deer figures are not the way contemporary artists would portray these animals, hence the confusion in knowing
which is the top of the picture. Central
Baja California, photo 1962.*

*4-13 Geometric petroglyphs,
viewable in many ways. Little Petroglyph Canyon, California. Photo
1988.*

*4-14 Petroglyph Point, Modoc
County, California. Simple geometric
elements may be viewed upside down
or sideways by persons who have not
seen the site and have only the photo
of the rock art. Photo Helen Crotty,
1972.*

IDENTIFICATION OF PHOTOS—INCLUDE:

• *Size scale*

• *Indicator of which way is up (or north arrow)*

• *Name of the site*

• **Size Scale,** 15 cm. (6 inches) to 30 cm. (12 inches) long: Alternate units can be marked off in solid black and white (a ruler may be used, but you will rarely be able to see the small markings or numbers on it). This scale can be hand-held in the picture if the rock surface is friable, or it can be attached to the rock with a bit of masking tape placed on the back (fig. 4-1). See previous cautions about tape on the rock art site.

• **"Up" or "North" Indicator.** A cardboard strip, cut to a point at one end, may be placed next to the rock art so that there is no confusion about which way the rock art is oriented (fig. 4-11). For rock art on a horizontal surface, the arrow can be used to point north and show the orientation of the flat rock on which the art occurs.

• **Name of Site.** The site designator (name or number) is easily written with heavy marking pens on a label, sometimes just a wide piece of white artist's tape, so that the information can be read in the photograph. A better label is a piece of white cardboard, about 3 by 8 inches in size, with a central horizontal line dividing it into halves: the upper half for a site name, the lower half for location (fig. 4-1). While recorders familiar with the site will also be familiar with abbreviations and cryptic symbols, the designations should be intelligible to anyone and not just the members of the field crew. For this reason, it is recommended that labels identify the *country* and the *state, county, or province,* as well as the name or number of the site. A site name does not give any information about the location, and even numbers in a standard system (like Riv-114) are meaningful only to those familiar with the state and county involved.

118

So if you are going to go to the trouble of putting identifiers in the photograph, let them be complete enough so that they can be understood by those who have never heard of your site or area.

The clever reader will no doubt have figured out that all of this information can be placed on a single six- or twelve-inch arrow, and that once made, it can be moved from element to element as the rock art is photographed. This is cheap, unobtrusive, and a great time-saver in the record keeping. The difference between having these identifiers and not having them, is the difference between a snapshot and a scientific record.

Some recorders also like to show the designation of the element being photographed, their name, the date, and other kinds of catalog information. However, the use of "message boards" and similar devices can clutter up the photograph so much as to overwhelm the subject of the picture. You want a picture of rock art, not a picture of a sign. A sign with a lot of detailed information will have to be photographed in a close-up to be legible, leaving little or no room for rock art in the same picture.

For illustration photos which may be reproduced in print at some future time, it is important to be able to crop out all the identifiers so that the photo shows only the rock art. Therefore, it is a good idea to put the identifiers in a corner which can be masked out if desired. **Those who plan ahead can handle this problem by taking two pictures: one with the identifiers and one without.**

If you use the identifiers mentioned above, you don't really need a catalog of your photographs. However, you may wish to keep a log which identifies your camera settings, lighting conditions, or other notes that you can use to improve future photography. You also may need to have notes which will allow you to link the photos with the drawings and other records you have taken. The box on the previous page: "All Photos Must Have" is a minimum list of essential data, but for the overall record you will want to include additional information in your notes and records. Prints, slides and negatives should also be identified with the name of the photographer, the date of the picture, and the site name and location.

It is an excellent procedure to label everything you get back from the photo processor with the key information. **This marking should be done on each individual slide, negative, and print, not merely the top one in a stack**—or worse, the box or envelope in which the photographs are kept and from which they are easily separated! Even in formal archives, like the Rock Art Archive at UCLA, it is distressing how often photographs turn up without any identification whatever. At one time, these were probably in labeled envelopes, but over the years the information has become separated from the photograph and made the picture largely worthless.

Slides and prints can be labeled with hand-written information (slow and tedious), or the process can be greatly speeded up by using rubber stamps or gummed labels. Negatives can be labeled with india ink or felt-tip pens, writing on the clear margin (emulsion or rough side). In spite of the small writing area available on slides and negatives, all of the important data can be directly affixed with care to the photo itself, thereby avoiding all future confusion from loss of notes or photo logs. While this is a rather boring chore, it is important and **it must be done immediately on receiving your photographic materials from the processor.** It is difficult enough to remember all the details the day the slides come back; it is impossible if you wait for months or years to get around to it. It goes without saying that the person who took the photographs is the person who can readily provide the identifications—if unlabeled pictures are passed on to someone else, most of the value of the photographic record may be lost.

If all the slides, negatives, and prints are individually labeled, the photo log serves merely as a catalog which may be very useful in keeping track of your records.

DRAWING THE ROCK ART ELEMENTS

Careful drawing of each rock art panel will provide the most accurate and comprehensive recording you will do at a site. Whereas lighting conditions or faded art may cause inadequate photographs, the careful observer can draw every detail. Drawing forces the recorder to examine designs at close range, noting in particular any superimpositions, subtle color differences, weathering and over-painting which may not show clearly in a photograph. Details discovered from such careful scrutiny should be noted on the drawing and in your notes.

A few guidelines for drawings are given here, but since every site is different, what works well in one location may not do so well in another. Many smaller sites have been recorded simply by making observational sketches of the rock art at the site. Others are best recorded with scale drawings. Some may require a series of rather complicated "roll-out" drawings, particularly if the rock art occurs on several faces of the same rock. Much rock art occurs on irregularly-shaped surfaces, and it is sometimes in places that are difficult to reach, such as high on a cliff or on the roof of a cave.

To begin the drawing task, label your newly completed sketch map with letters or numbers to designate the individual faces or panels where the rock art elements appear (fig. 4-15). Now your sketch map has become not only a layout of the site, but an index drawing to the places where the rock art occurs.

The goal for a complete recording of the rock art is to make a sketch drawing of all the individual elements at the site. However, if this is not possible because of the time required, examples of the different artistic elements at the site can be drawn as a kind of "catalog" of what is there (fig. 4-16). Some sites contain a tremendous number of repetitive elements—for example, dozens or even hundreds of circles or hand prints. Unless there is time to deal with each of these individually, it may be

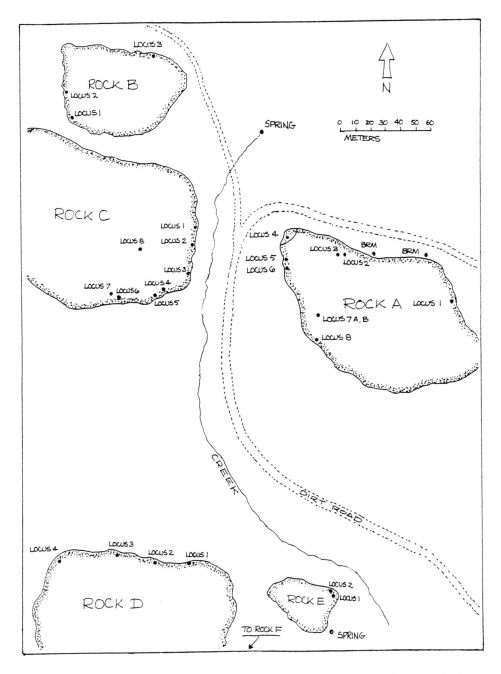

4-15 An excellent and neat sketch map showing the layout of a rock art site (see discussion of mapping in Chapter 3). Only one bit of information is missing: THE NAME OF THE SITE. No matter how carefully the record is done, if it applies to an unidentified location it loses all value.

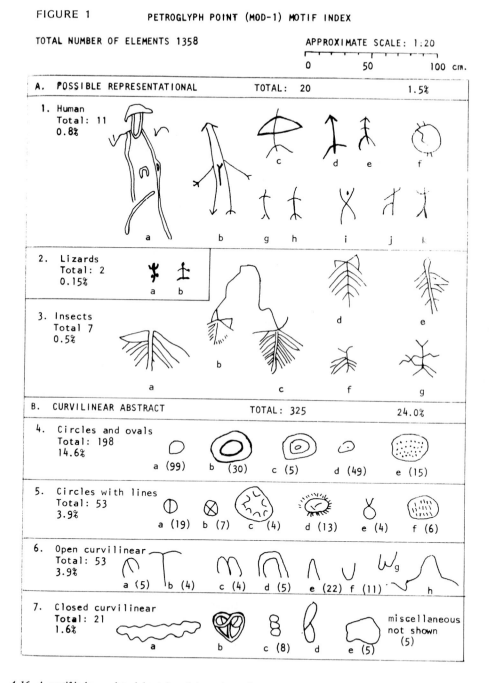

4-16 A motif index, a pictorial catalog of the rock art elements found at site Mod-1, Petroglyph Point in Modoc County, California. This is not the complete index for the site, but shows the difficulty of dealing with many simple geometric elements. Reproduced from Crotty, 1981.

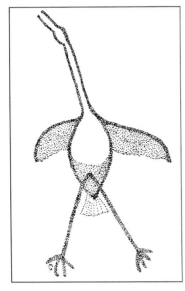

4-17 Bird, central Baja California petroglyph site. Stipple technique requires patience but reproduces well the peck marks of the petroglyph and shows the areas with lighter and heavier workmanship. Most initial field sketches are not this detailed, but a careful recorder will get all the information needed to make an ink drawing of this quality. Drawing by Esther Schwartz.

possible to draw only a few examples. Indicate in the notes how many such figures are present, and their variability (in size, color, and grouping on the rocks). For a "phase 1" report, it is probably better to draw the rock art in this way than to start at one end of the site and have to quit after recording a few rocks in meticulous detail, leaving no time to say anything about the majority of the art.

Many recorders feel that they lack artistic ability and cannot produce reliable drawings of rock art. However, the objective is to produce sketches, not works of art. Indeed, creative art is not wanted since you are merely recording what is there, not making your own artistic statement. It is true that some recorders draw better than others, but this is not a function of artistic ability. It has to do with neatness, accuracy, and the ability to see the rock art (fig. 4-17). There are, of course, individual variations in these qualities, but anyone who can see what is on the rock can make a reasonably reliable drawing of it. The pointers below should help.

• **Show the elements as they were originally.** Drawing rock art elements one by one seems a simple and even tedious clerical task, and sometimes it is. However, anyone who actually does it finds that it is more complex than it appears. Fading, weathering, irregular rock surfaces, and superimpositions of later pictures all make it difficult to see the rock art.

Recorders sometimes have problems determining how best to represent rock art that has deteriorated due to natural or human causes. If they are so scientific and literal-minded that they draw only the paint remaining

124

on the wall, they will have to omit every place where part of a line or surface has spalled off or weathered away. This can be done very exactly, but if a site is extremely weathered, the recording of scattered splotches of paint may not give any idea at all of what the rock art originally looked like. It may create a "connect the dots" picture which is so confusing that the record shows literally nothing but scattered dots and blotches of paint. Of course, the recorders do this to avoid making guesses and injecting their own reconstruction into the pictures. On the other hand, observers at the site can see far more than researchers looking at such a field sketch. For example, if recorders have drawn forty pictures of rabbits at the site, all of which are represented in a standard way, when they come upon a weathered and partial picture of a rabbit they ought to be able to see that this is another rabbit picture. They can show this in their drawing, using solid colors for what is actually remaining and some sort of shading or dotted lines to indicate what they think is missing. If this is not done, the partial picture of a rabbit becomes a new kind of picture at the site and will enter into all the statistics as something very different from what it really was when the artist painted the original picture. This example is an actual case, where records of a rock art site in Baja California include pictures of rabbits and also some geometrical figures (ovals and paired ovals) in the list of artistic elements at the site. Further field investigation showed that the latter were actually the ears of rabbits—the recorder saw these but did not recognize the fainter parts of the drawing which show the rabbits' bodies.

The opposite extreme from recording minute spots of paint is equally to be avoided. Some "artistes" want to create their own imaginary rendering of the art, adding embellishments and missing details. They come up with a finished picture that actually falsifies the record. The proper approach is somewhere between these two extremes, and this is what makes the clerical task of recording a difficult one in many sites. The only solution is to show in your drawings and notes what is actually there, and also to indicate on your field record what you think the picture looked like when the ancient artist left it. Accompany your drawing with a good photograph (fig. 4-18). It will be a big help in aiding future workers to understand and interpret your record. If you are lucky, you will come upon a site where the art is bright, pristine, and free of confusions—such sites do

Petroglyph Record   7∠

Date 3·12·76 Recorder JACK SCHWARTZ   Rock # 43   Sect. 6   to Ⓝ
                                                   AREA A

No. of decorated faces 1   Dimensions of decorated faces. A. 3.0 M. HIGH X 3.5 M. WIDE. APPROX

Method of Decoration
☒ Pecked
☐ Rubbed grooves

B. _____
C. _____
D. _____

Kind of rock: A B C D Other

Natural weathering: A (B) C

Superimposition:

	Suggested	made	made By
Rubbing			
mold			
Photograph			
Specimen			

Element Over Elements

13	→	14
	→	
	→	
	→	

Indicate North   Face: Indicate North   WEST Face:

Design Elements

Scale

4-18 *Rock art recording form with attached photograph of same site. Central Baja California. Record by Jack Schwartz, 1976.*

exist but they are unfortunately a small minority.

   * Record the entire panel of art. The spatial arrangement of the elements of art at a site also is extremely important to record since context and assemblages of elements may assist in making interpretations of the meaning and significance of the motifs. This is where your sketch map becomes very useful. You can mark on the map the individual assemblages of rock art such as panels of associated figures, or individual boulders in a boulder field (see fig. 4-15), marking each of these areas on the map with a letter or number which can serve as a key to your drawings. This will show the overall spatial relationships of the art at the site and will allow identification of clustering of certain elements in particular areas of the site.

   Each drawing should ideally record the entire panel (figs. 4-19, 4-20b), showing the spatial relationships between the individual elements. This can be done with a sketch showing measurements, but the easiest way to show the spatial relationships is to draw the elements to scale on a piece of graph paper, locating each element with respect to the others and to the rock surfaces (fig. 4-21a,b). By using a suitable scale on your graph paper, you can measure in the sizes and arrangement of the individual elements of the panel by using a tape measure. It helps immensely if two people work together on this, with one making the measurements and the other doing the drawing. One person can do it alone, but slowly—two people can do it rapidly and well. Three or more people tend to get in each other's way. If you are fortunate enough to have a large crew of recorders, the most efficient way to use them is to divide up the site area and let teams of two people record different areas.

   Recording superimpositions is important. Where any part of a drawing is on top of another, a note should be made of which element is below and which is on top. There are sometimes dozens or hundreds of such superimpositions in a site. Inaccessible rock art which cannot be closely approached to make a drawing may have to be recorded by using a series of telephoto photographs and overlapping them to create a composite view. Rarely, rock art is done in a *bas relief* which is difficult to draw,

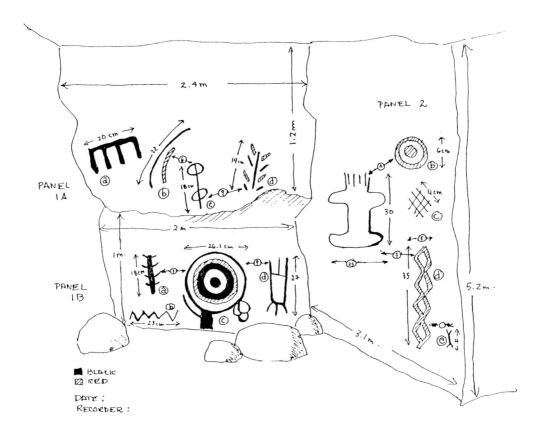

4-19 *Field drawing showing panels of associated figures at a rock art site in southern California. The drawing shows colors, dimensions, and relationships but does not indicate the date, the recorder, or the designation of the site. Even if the drawing is in a published report, it should show all of the basic information and should stand alone, without reference to other notes or records.*

4-20a *Photo taken ca. 1900 at "Picture Rock," site in Fayette County, Pennsylvania, on the east bank of the Monongahela River overlooking Millsboro. The site is now destroyed. Print no. 5033 in the collection of the Carnegie Museum, Pittsburgh.*

4-20b *Drawing of the same rock, originally published by the American Philosophical Society in 1888. A motif index could be compiled from this detailed drawing. The only missing basic information is the sequence of superimpositions; many are shown but which element is the later one cannot be determined from either photo or drawing. Illustrations courtesy of James L. Swauger.*

129

4-21a, b Comparison of photo and drawing of rock art at Selby Rocks, Carrizo Plain, California.
Because of dark patination on the rock as well as weathering, the drawing on graph paper is far more informative in this case than the photograph which failed to record many details visible to the recorder. The white areas in the photo (marked "exf" on the drawing) are places where the rock surface has exfoliated. Drawing by Tom Sanger, 1980.

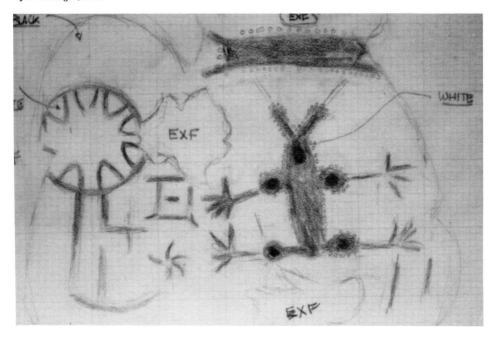

130

but the problem has been solved by Georgia Lee and her crew, who have recorded dozens of these panels on Easter Island (fig. 4-22a, b).

AIDS TO SIMPLIFY
THE DRAWING PROCESS

Various devices have been used to speed up the drawing of rock art without the time-consuming task of measuring each element individually. One approach, developed independently in Australia, the United States, and no doubt other countries as well, is to build a frame of wood or small-diameter plastic pipe (PVC) with a grid of strings attached to it at about 6-inch intervals. The recorder places the grid over the rock art and then draws the rock art in the squares of the grid on corresponding squares of graph paper. However, such a grid works well only on relatively flat surfaces. If the rock is irregular or has projections, you cannot get a rigid grid to lie flat against the rock art.

String Grid. This problem has been overcome at some sites by developing a flexible grid, which is a net of string, attached directly to the rock art face with tape (figs. 4-23 to 4-25). The tape is never put directly on top of any rock art, but only on parts of the surface that are undecorated. The advantage of a flexible grid is that you can set the lines at measured intervals as close together as necessary, depending on the size of the rock art elements to be drawn. The grid can be placed on the rock quickly and accurately, by first placing two perpendicular strings across the middle of the art. If the rock art is on a vertical face, you can use a weight at the bottom of each string to hold it perpendicular, and tape it down at the ends. Then, working toward the edges of the design area, the vertical strings are placed at measured intervals and taped down on undecorated surfaces. Cross strings are added, using a line level to insure that they are horizontal. If the rock art is on a horizontal surface, it is much easier to measure the grid and tape down the strings. Once in place, the grid makes it possible to draw complex rock art accurately and rapidly, sketching the various elements on a two-dimensional piece of graph paper even though the rock art may be on an irregular three-dimensional surface. It is also possible to prepare a net of the desired mesh size in advance. Be sure to

4-22a, b   Comparison of photo and drawing of rock art at Orongo, Easter Island.
4-22a   Photo 1983.

132

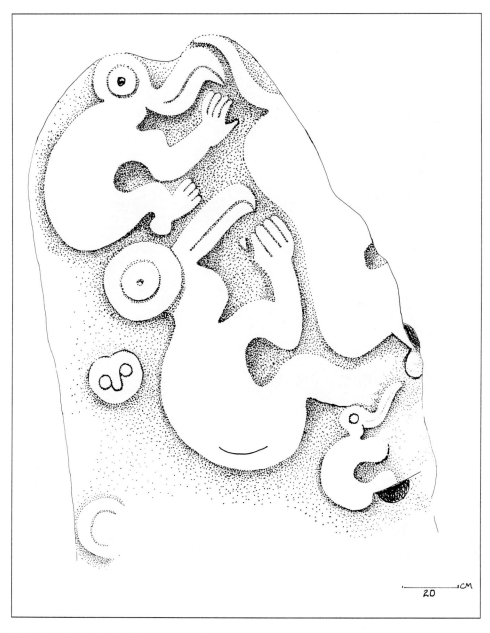

4-22b, Drawing by Esther Schwartz, same element as 4-22a. This is one of few areas of the world where rock art is produced in relief, with the backgrounds pecked away rather than the images. The outstanding stipple drawing is far more informative than the photo due to weathering and discoloration of the rock surface.

133

4-23 to 4-25   Use of string grid to aid in drawing rock art images. The reference strings make it easy to transfer the elements to graph paper in their proper relationships and proportions. The string is attached with bits of masking tape which can be readily removed. For rock art on sloping or vertical faces, a line level is used to make the cross strings horizontal.

4-23   Grid on rock art face at La Española, Costa Rica. Photo 1979.

4-24   Grid on horizontal rock surface at Rano Kau, Easter Island. Photo 1983.

4-25   Gridding a large petroglyph on a boulder, Easter Island. Photo 1983.

134

use netting knots or sew the string connections. The wrong ties at the corners will cause the knots to slip and the mesh to become irregular in shape. You also have to be careful not to stretch or distort the net when attaching it to the rock.

Depending on the areal extent of the rock art, a simpler method is to attach a horizontal string across the rock art (fig. 4-26). Use a grease pencil or felt pen to mark the string at intervals. Use a line level to make it horizontal if the surface is sloping or vertical. Put this reference line on the graph paper, and draw everything in relationship to the horizontal line. An even easier method is simply to attach some very small bits of drafting tape to the rock, arranged in a horizontal line at regular intervals (fig. 4-26). These provide a reference scale which can be used as a guide to the drawing. When you are through recording, be sure to remove all tape completely.

Most tape will not adhere to moist rock, or even to some dry rocks such as sandstone. Many varieties of tape have been tried with varying results:

> **Drafting tape.** Will often do the job and is easily and completely removed.
> **Scotch tape.** Generally not very good, but the heavier type with embedded threads (filament tape) seems to work best on most surfaces.
> **Adhesive tape.** Sometimes works; difficult to remove without leaving adhesive on the rock.
> **Freezer tape.** Generally unsatisfactory.
> **Pipe tape.** Used to wrap gas pipe lines, it is very strong, wide, and easily removed. Expensive and does not adhere to all kinds of rock.
> **Duct tape.** Silver-colored tape used for wrapping air duct lines. It is wide, strong, and generally effective on sandstone and basalt but less useful on other kinds of rock.

In sum, most kinds of tape will work sometimes, but filament tape and duct tape seem to have the best holding power on rock surfaces. Whatever tape you use, be sure that it can be easily and completely removed

4-26   Making a scale drawing using a horizontal string (set with a line level) and bits of masking tape spaced at regular intervals. La Española, Costa Rica. Photo Joan Seibert, 1979.

when you are finished with your drawing, and do not leave it on the rock any longer than necessary. Most tape is readily removable if it is peeled off within a few hours, but becomes difficult to remove if left on the rock for an extended period when it becomes "baked on" by the sun.

A flexible grid also can be made by using a large sheet of plastic with a grid drawn on it (fig. 4-27). This creates a transparent piece of large graph paper which is taped in place over the rock art. A cheap, clear plastic drop-cloth used by painters is good because it is very light weight. The grid is put on the plastic in advance using a felt-tipped marker pen which writes on plastic. Keep these pens away from the rock art since they also write on rock very easily. Most such pens have waterproof ink which dries instantly, so it is next to impossible to remove accidental marks on the rock. Advantages of the plastic grid are that it can be prepared in advance, is flexible and conforms to the surface of the rock, and takes much less time to set up than a string grid.

136

This method has a few problems. You may need some patient assistants to hold the plastic grid over the rock art while you make the drawing, duplicating what you see in the large plastic grid onto your small scale graph paper. It is usually necessary to tape the plastic in place, however,

4-27 Use of a plastic grid over the rock art to aid in making scale drawing. The sheet of plastic is marked with a marking pen and the individual squares are lettered and numbered (A-1, A-2, etc.) to correspond with a similarly-marked grid on the graph paper drawing. The very light-weight plastic is held to the rock using tape. Site Riv-114, Riverside County, California, 1986.

which is why a very light-weight plastic is desirable. Large pieces of light plastic are impossible to handle in windy areas or on large overhangs. In addition, depending on lighting conditions, there may be such a glare off the plastic that you can't see the rock art underneath, particularly if faint elements are present. This can sometimes be reduced by using a plastic drop cloth which has a matte rather than a shiny surface; both are readily available at paint supply stores. Polaroid sun glasses can also help to eliminate sun high-lights from the plastic and enable you to see the rock art.

Plastic sheets of this kind can also be used to make tracings as discussed in Chapter 5.

All of these recording methods have proven to be effective time-savers at some sites and more trouble than they are worth at other sites. They are merely aids. You will still need to do a certain amount of measuring with a ruler and checking individual elements before the drawings are completed. However, each method will help produce a sketch that shows the correct size and spacing of the rock art elements.

IMPORTANT REMINDER—If you've been reading carefully, you know that each and every drawing must have on it:

- *The name of the site*
- *A size scale*
- *The recorder's name*
- *Date the record was made*

Indicate a north arrow for rock art on horizontal surfaces and be sure that every drawing of vertical surfaces shows which way is up. For most rock art, there is nothing in the art itself to tell you which way is up and no way for future workers to know this unless you indicate it clearly, either with an arrow indicating "up" or a notation marking the top of the drawing. There is a legion of published rock art drawings which are printed upside down or turned 90 degrees. Even if the art portrays human or animal forms, there is no certainty that a prehistoric artist followed our convention of putting the head end at the top. Many life forms are portrayed in rock art sideways or upside down from the way our artists would represent them. Furthermore, such figures may be oriented every which way even within one site. This is partly a function of the difficulty of producing images on rocks rather than flat pieces of paper, and partly a function of the stylistic conventions of the ancient artists. Photographs are generally easier to orient since they will often include a bush, a person, or some other obvious indicator of which way is up. However, detailed photographs of individual elements have the same problem as drawings (figs.

4-12 to 4-14), and such photographs also get printed upside down in numerous publications. The correct orientation of drawings may often be verified by reference to photographs, if the recorder forgot to mark the drawing to show the top. The reverse is also true—in cases where the drawing is marked to show which way is up, it may orient photographs which lack an "up" marker. To check drawings against photographs, it is often possible to project a color slide on a piece of paper the size of the drawing and make a direct comparison.

Drawing the rock art is, for the most part, an easy and enjoyable task, and is by no means as difficult as it may sound from all the pointers above. Very little rock art is too complicated for a novice recorder to reproduce on paper. Even bas reliefs can be drawn (see fig. 4-22b). The time required for drawings depends on the size of the site and the complexity of the art, but many small sites can be entirely drawn in only a day or two. Rock art is seldom intricate or detailed because of the limitations of the brushes, paints, or chipping tools used by the original artists. Much rock art is composed of geometric figures (disks, checkerboards, and lines) and various life forms drawn as simple stick figures. Shading and subtle detail are rarely present.

If you have completed a properly labeled sketch map, drawings, and notes, you have done a job of documentation that is better than that done by many professionals, and in fact is a rarity in rock art recording. Your record will be appreciated by all future workers who have the need to consult your findings. However, a part of the record that may be even more important consists of photographs of the rock art, as discussed previously. While drawings can record information not seen in a photograph, the reverse is also true and it allows a check on the accuracy of the recorder's drawings. There are numerous instances in which photographs show that the accompanying drawings are entirely incorrect. A complete record will therefore include both drawings and photographs. If there is time to do only one of these, it is probably best to concentrate on the photographic record.

MODIFICATIONS TO THE ROCK ART
TO MAKE A RECORD POSSIBLE

Since our interest is to preserve the record, it is common sense to avoid all physical impact to the rock art and to do nothing which will alter the record or confuse it for future researchers.

As an example of unnecessary impacts, there are a number of rock art sites in the world which have every panel and sometimes every individual element marked with an obtrusive number, letter, or other catalog device, sometimes painted on the rock, sometimes actually chiselled into the rock surface (fig. 4-28). There is never any need for this kind of vandalism. If it is necessary to go back and find specific elements at a site, this is easily dealt with by notes and photographs and it is not necessary to leave physical marks at the site.

CHALKING

Another all too common impact on the rock art is the use of chalk to mark out petroglyphs. Endless pages of debate have been written about the benefits and evils of such practices. Even some painted pictographs have been obtrusively chalked, with an unnecessary outline drawn around elements in a perfectly clear and obvious painting. With the development of dating methods that depend upon the chemistry of the patination and the rock surface, there may be serious damage to future research by adding any chemical substances to rock art elements.

An important objection to the use of chalk or any other enhancement technique is that it may not accurately portray the rock art. If the rock art can't be seen without chalking, how can the chalk be put in the right places? Even if the chalking is accurate, the viewer of the resulting record has no way of knowing whether the art was created by prehistoric people or whether it includes incorrect renderings or guesswork made by a recent recorder.

In spite of these appropriate cautions and reservations, for some older sites now destroyed, the sin of chalking has given us a far better documentation of the rock art than we would otherwise have (see figs. 4-29a, b). However, we do not recommend chalking rock art. In special circumstances, it may be necessary to enhance faint petroglyphs with a chemically

4-28   An example of "scientific vandalism" in which recorders of the site marked each panel by applying their own designations (IX-A in upper left). Is this necessary for recording? It is not uncommon and such marking is found in many locations around the world. Neolithic rock art site at Abka, Sudan, flooded when the new Aswan Dam was built. Photo 1960.

neutral paste of flour and water, which is washed off after the record is made (see discussion below).

**WATER TO
ENHANCE
PAINTINGS**

For painted rock art, there is little that can be done to enhance the

4-29a, b   Two views of same petroglyph panel on rock slab from eastern U.S. (now in a museum). The height of the photographed area is about 70 cm.
Photos courtesy of James L. Swauger.

4-29a   The rock without enhancement.

4-29b   The panel with the petroglyphs enhanced with chalk. Although this book recommends against any impacts to the rock art, and most recorders condemn chalking of rock art, it has to be conceded that there are exceptions to every rule, and in this example the information in the chalked photograph is useful and little can be discerned in the other picture. An equally good enhancement of the rock art might be obtainable from proper lighting and good photography. It is also possible to preserve the details through other records such as tracings or rubbings.

142

images. Certainly no material of any kind should be put on top of the paint. There has been a practice, by some recorders, of using a spray bottle to dampen faint painted elements. This is believed to darken the paint, improve the contrast, and hence make it possible to draw the art more accurately. In places where every rain causes water to run over the rock art, this practice can do little damage. In dry caves the situation is different, and the practice of using water is strongly condemned by Van Rijssen (1987) who reviews the negative effects (physical and chemical) which may result from adding water to a dry surface. If the drawing can be seen, there is no need for spraying. If it cannot be seen, the addition of water rarely improves the image enough to aid in the recording. Furthermore, observation of this technique in use shows that people with a spray bottle in hand have a tendency to spray the same element several times, since whatever enhancement effect is present will last only a few minutes, often not long enough to make the drawing. A much better approach is to try photographic methods of enhancement, either by use of filters or a head-on flash picture which can often reveal more details than are readily visible.

However, the statement that spraying is almost never justified does not mean that it is *never* justified. If the rock art is too faint to record, it has already deteriorated so far that the use of water cannot be said to be the cause of destruction—is it better to get the record or simply leave the rock art to disappear without further recording effort?

It remains true that in some instances it is impossible to make any record, either drawings or photographs, without doing something to the site. There are times when one has to balance the need for a record against the risk of unforeseen damage to the site. In other words, while unnecessary impacts are always to be avoided, there may be some occasions on which impacts are necessary. Unfortunately, it is also true that there are many sites for which impacts don't matter. If the site is destined to be at the bottom of a reservoir shortly, it is just fussiness to worry about chalking, spraying, or other impacts by the recorder. Here it is not the impacts that matter, but the accuracy and completeness of the record, since the task is a last opportunity for ever getting *any* documentation of the site.

REMOVING SOIL
AND VEGETATION
FROM THE ART

A rock art representation is partially buried by alluviation, rock fall, or accumulation of midden against the rock art. Do you dig away the covering material so you can record the rock art? Or do you quit with a fragmentary record? Some very important sites would not be known at all unless sand, leaf-mold, or similar debris had been removed so that the rock art became visible. On the other hand, if part of the rock art is buried in midden representing an archaeological deposit, the rock art recorder cannot dig under the surface without violating antiquities regulations. The best advice here is to consult an archaeologist if there is any indication that some of the rock art is buried, and avoid any digging or removal of surface material from the site. See the code of ethics of ARARA (Appendix D).

A related problem occurs in tropical areas where the rock art is not buried, but may be entirely concealed by moss or other vegetation. At one tropical site in Costa Rica, removal of the moss revealed some very shallow petroglyphs which could not be seen at all until the vegetation was removed. Even then, they were so faint that they were difficult to photograph or draw in detail (fig. 4-30a, b). To enhance the visibility of other elements at the same site, the recorders painted the grooves with a paste made of flour and water (chalk was not used because it is not chemically neutral and the rock was limestone). This allowed for good photographs of some very complex panels containing multiple elements (fig. 4-31a). Rock art elements at the site which were deeply cut into the rock, however, were not touched because it was not necessary to do anything to them to get both drawings and photographs in ample detail. Photographs taken at repeat visits, two and nine years later, showed that nearly all of the "enhancement" had been washed away by the tropical rain and that many of the elements were again invisible and beginning to become overgrown

***4-30a, b Two views of limestone ledge at La Española, Costa Rica. The petroglyphs (arrows)
were entirely concealed under moss and could not be seen until the moss was scraped away.***
*4-30a Panel before recording.   4-30b Rock art elements revealed as moss is removed. The recorder is at-
tached to a safety line since the rocks in this wet tropical area are very slippery and a fall (to a river many feet
below) would be disastrous. Photos 1979.*

4-31a, b *Two views of same rock art panel at the site of La Española, Costa Rica.* *4-31a , the panel as recorded in 1979, after moss was removed and the petroglyphs were enhanced with a paste of flour and water. 4-31b The same rock art photographed in 1988. The enhancements have been washed away by tropical rains and moss is again growing in the petroglyph grooves. Photo Rita Shepard.*

146

with moss once more.

From what has been said, it should be clear that the recording of a site (whether drawings or photographs) is very much affected by lighting. Rather than deciding to "enhance" the art, experienced recorders often find that to see it better, all that is necessary is to wait until the lighting changes, or to use one of the photographic techniques (such as filters).   It is a last resort to use any other enhancements. Recorders who revisit rock art sites find that they frequently discover new rock art that they did not see at their first visit. This is often simply a function of the time of day or season of the year, with different lighting conditions that make previously obscure elements suddenly become clearly visible.

5

ADDITIONAL RECORDING TECHNIQUES

If you have followed the preceding recording steps, you have done a good job of scientifically documenting your rock art site. Some additional techniques are discussed in this chapter which are not essential to the recording effort but may be useful in some cases. Handled with care, these recording techniques provide a life-size record of the art and depict the exact relationships of the rock art elements to one another. While we do not suggest the frequent use of these procedures, we have included them here because we want you to know the correct techniques and possible pitfalls if you feel that your site merits these additional kinds of records.

No attempt should be made to create any copy or replica which involves the risk of physical damage to the rock art. Some rock art sites have been heavily damaged by failed attempts to make casts, molds, or other copies involving the application of some substance (plaster, fiberglass, latex) to the rock art. Any attempts in this direction require real expertise. Damage to rock art sites is a violation of antiquities laws.

The two techniques discussed below, if used properly, will have little impact on a rock art site. They are not ordinarily part of basic recording, however, and do not substitute for the photos and drawings discussed in Chapter 4.

TRACINGS

Tracings are made by using a clear, flexible plastic or acetate film and waterproof marking pens (fig. 5-1). The plastic is placed over the petroglyph/pictograph and secured with masking or duct tape. **Tape is not placed on top of any rock art, and all of it is carefully and completely removed after the tracing is done.** In some cases, no tape will stick to the rock and one or more assistants will have to hold the plastic sheet in place. This is particularly difficult if the rock art is on an overhang or the ceiling of a cave, or when the rock has a very irregular surface.

5-1 Rock art recording by making a tracing of the rock art on a sheet of plastic. On this site, the red and black colors of the pictographs can be approximated by using red and black marker pens to make the tracing. Riv-114, Riverside County, California. Photo 1986.

Small pieces of plastic are available in many forms from art supply houses. You need plastic which is flexible enough to conform to the rock surface, yet transparent enough so you can see through it. A plastic with a slightly matte surface is easier to see through if there is a problem with reflected light. Polaroid sunglasses also help, and the simple trick of

150

patience (waiting until the light angle has changed, as mentioned in the previous chapter) will allow you to see the rock art elements more clearly.

In some cases, you may need a large sheet of plastic, several feet on a side. Indeed, tracings are of value primarily in recording large areas with many rock art designs, so that the overall composition can be seen. Unless the individual rock art elements are very complex, tracings are not of much value. Individual elements can be reproduced adequately from drawings, notes, and photographs. Painters' transparent plastic drop cloths (available at any paint or hardware store) are inexpensive and will cover large art panels because they are commonly 9 by 12 feet in size. They are also very light weight. This is a disadvantage because they can be torn fairly easily, but they take a very small amount of storage space and can be folded small enough to be kept in a large manila envelope. They are also easier to attach to the rock surface than more durable, thicker, and heavier plastic sheets.

With the plastic sheet over the rock art, secured by tape or held by assistants, recorders make a tracing of the visible rock art using *water-proof* marking pens. The tracing can be done very rapidly, but it must be a faithful reproduction of what is actually there. Watch out for holes or tears in the plastic which would allow the marking pen to mark the rock. You might want to make guesses about missing lines or parts of figures in your notes, but *a tracing is a literal reproduction of what is on the rock and should not include details which are not visible.* Hence, if you add lines or details which you provide to show what you believe the original picture looked like, be sure that your additions are clearly discriminated from the marks that are visible on the rock. This differentiation can be done by using dotted lines or some other convention for noting your reconstruction effort.

Marking pens come in a variety of colors, and since the majority of painted rock art is done in black, red, orange or yellow, and white, use of marking pens in these colors can approximate not only the drawings, but their colors as well. White can be shown by outlining the painted lines in black, but unless this procedure is clearly explained on the drawing, it can confuse the viewer who sees only the black outline.

Once the tracing is roughed out, it can be laid flat and checked against the rock art for corrections or minor details which need to be added. The tracing then has to be marked with all of the **essential identifiers: site name, designation for the section of the site being recorded, date, recorder's name, and which way is up.** For tracings of surfaces which are near horizontal, a **north arrow** should be included. All this information can be written in a corner of the plastic sheet with marking pens. You can also add any special notes explaining details that might not be clear from the drawing. For example, if you indicate elements painted in white paint by outlining a blank area in black, the viewer needs to be told of your procedure. A key should be provided to any conventions you have used to represent color, shading, or superimpositions. Once all of the ink is dry (virtually instantaneous with marking pens), then carefully fold the plastic and put it into a labeled envelope. Plastic tracings several feet on a side can fit into a 9 by 12 manila envelope for cataloging and filing.

One of the most effective uses of plastic tracings is to take a photographic slide of the tracing. Later, you can project this slide onto a piece of paper to use as the basis for a scale drawing that shows each element in correct relationship and proportion. The tracing allows the transfer of an irregular surface to a flat surface and therefore avoids the very difficult problem of making projections of concave or convex surfaces on which rock art often occurs. Sometimes a slide of the plastic tracing is an invaluable supplement to the actual slides of the site, since the tracing has no distortions of perspective and can clearly show elements which may be only faintly visible in a photograph.

To summarize, the plastic tracing is a valuable supplementary record, but it is not a routine recording method. Its value is in recording panels, assemblages, or "scenes" in which there are several parts making up the overall picture. **It is not a substitute for notes,** and indeed, may require considerable written observations, particularly if there is reason to believe that some of the drawings in the assemblage are of a different age than others.

Tracings also have limited utility for recording petroglyphs although some effective tracings have been made of incised or pecked elements. For petroglyphs, however, a better visual impression can be gained from another technique:

RUBBINGS

Rubbings of petroglyphs are made by using wax on cloth or rice paper (figs. 5-2, 5-3b). They make a negative copy of the rock art design by showing the highest portions in dark color and the engraved or pecked areas in lighter color. This is a recording technique that has long been used by individuals seeking a duplicate of monuments, plaques, tombstones, and similar remains which bear relief inscriptions or pictures. Sometimes rubbings are the only way that shallow-grooved petroglyphs can be clearly discerned. In these cases, rubbings are an essential part of the recording process.

It is unlikely that any damage to rock art will result from one properly made rubbing. Rubbings are most often made, however, to obtain reproductions for display. It is possible that repeated rubbings could wear away the rock, particularly if it is soft, such as sandstone. Rubbings, like other impacts to rock art, should be done only when they serve a useful purpose.

One serious potential source of damage is the production of rubbings using printer's ink, paint, or other chemical substances which can soak through the cloth or paper onto the rock art. For this reason, only reasonably dry cakes of rubbing material should be used to apply the pigment, because these will not come in direct contact with the rock art.

To make a rubbing, scrape a dry cake of rubbing wax across the surface of a piece of cloth or paper held on top of the rock art. It takes a bit

5-2 *Rock art recording by making a rubbing on cloth. This works well with petroglyphs that are deeply cut into the rock. La Española, Costa Rica. Photos 1979.*

5-3a *A deeply cut petroglyph at La Española, Costa Rica.*

5-3b *The same petroglyph with cloth affixed for rubbing.*

154

of practice to develop the correct light touch, but it is easy to see that where the rock is directly in contact with the cloth (the high spots), lots of pigment will be deposited, and where the rock is not touching the cloth (the low spots), little or no pigment will be rubbed on the cloth. The petroglyph grooves will appear as light lines on a darker background. Since petroglyphs are usually made by a pecking process that leaves many little indentations in the rock, a well-done rubbing will reproduce the texture of this manufacturing process very well, giving a good visual impression of the technique as well as the design.

If cloth is used, it should be a non-stretch variety for obvious reasons (cotton is good), and it should not be too thick or heavy. Pieces of an old cotton sheet are very good for this purpose. The artistic recorder will want to buy cloth which approximates the color of the rocks. If rice paper is used, it is usually necessary to dampen it and press it onto the surface of the rock. The pigment is applied after the paper dries.

Many types of wax pigment have been used for making rubbings. Kits of colored wax are sold for this purpose by art supply houses. Ordinary crayons are often effective, particularly the oversized ones of large diameter that are used by carpenters. They are available at lumber yards and builders' supply houses. Wax shoe polish works well too (almost dry and applied lightly with a shoe-polish brush—don't get it on the rock art).

Natural pits or holes in the surface of the rock will appear to be parts of the rock art in a rubbing. They can be removed from the rubbing by moving the cloth to a smooth area of the rock and filling in the blank "holes" by rubbing those areas again. Other imperfections which can be recognized as part of the rock surface, such as cracks, can be left in the rubbing as part of the reproduction.

Once the rubbing is finished, it should be laid flat and checked against the rock art for corrections or minor details which need to be added. Rubbings, too, have to be marked with all of the **essential identifiers: site name, designation for the section of the site being recorded, date,**

recorder's name, and which way is up. For rubbings of surfaces which are near horizontal, a north arrow should be included. It is repetitious to give this advice again, since it has been said more than once previously, but there is a reason: the overly large number of records in our files which omit some or all of this essential information and therefore are rendered useless. In the case of rubbings, all this information can be written unobtrusively in a corner of the rubbing, or it can be put on the back of the rubbing if it won't show through.

Unlike plastic tracings which can be put into envelopes and stored in relatively little space, cloth rubbings require more storage space. The Rock Art Archive at UCLA has hundreds of rubbings which are carefully filed. Yet, for purposes of the scholarly record, rubbings are less useful and the Archive would prefer fewer of them. Making rubbings should not be considered a routine recording procedure. Like tracings, rubbings should be reserved for complex elements or panels, petroglyphs which are so faint they cannot be recorded effectively any other way, or petroglyphs which are clearly of so much interest or aesthetic value that they merit display in a museum.

Note that some jurisdictions specifically prohibit the making of rubbings because of potential damage to the rock art. In general, permission to record a rock art site does not include permission to make rubbings, and this has to be negotiated separately. The problems occur where the rock art is heavily visited and where there are artistic elements which have display or souvenir value. Restrictions on the making of rubbings are in effect for many sites in the Southwestern U.S., all sites on federal property, and even places as distant as Easter Island. As usual, it is the abuses of a few, who have sometimes made hundreds of rubbings of the same petroglyph for commercial purposes, that compel restrictions.

ALUMINUM FOIL IMPRESSIONS

An unusual method of getting a replica of petroglyphs is reported by Steinbring and Farvour (1987). These workers used sheets of aluminum foil which were pressed into all cavities of the petroglyph. A Q-tip was used to press in the foil, although other reasonably soft but firm implements could serve for this purpose—the eraser end of a pencil, for example.

Once produced, the foil sheet needs to be mounted on cardboard, and it can then be stored flat with some padding to avoid crushing the impression. The authors feel that this is a more reliable method than the making of rubbings, because the aluminum foil produces an exact replica of the details of the pecking process, whereas the rubbing will not show as much detail. They see the foil reproductions as better because foil lacks color and texture "...which may confuse the image." Further, they report that the foil replicas allow for excellent photographs of the petroglyphs, free of the difficulties that may result from varying rock colors, water stains, and similar confusions.

This method, like the others mentioned above, is not something that should be routinely used for all the rock art in a site. Indeed, it would create a major storage problem if all the petroglyphs in a large rock art site were treated in this way. However, for examples of the technique and style, it may be desirable to produce some foil replicas along with other records. In the case of sites destined for destruction, the foil replicas would provide an excellent basis for exact reconstruction of petroglyphs in a museum. It is likely that such replicas could also be used for making casts of the rock art as well, since they form ready-made molds. Such a cast could do no damage to the rock art since the cast would be made from the aluminum-foil replica.

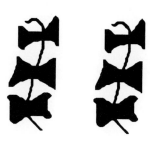

6

INTERPRETATIONS
AND DATING

Since the aim of this manual is to improve recording and documentation, the issues of interpretation are not discussed here in detail. That would require another whole book. However, anyone who has looked carefully at the images made by ancient artists cannot fail to wonder about the age and meaning of the rock art. Who made it? How old is it? Is there a message of some kind here, and if so, is it possible for us to figure out that message? These fascinating but difficult questions require a great deal of study and thought, and the answers vary depending upon the site under analysis.

INTERPRETING ROCK ART

Interpretation is only as good as the evidence of the rock art itself, and if that evidence is not fully and carefully recorded, there is no way for an interpretation to be valid. Certainly any interpretation that is offered has to be in conformity with the evidence before our eyes, and leaping to conclusions after looking at only a small number of the elements at a rock art site can only be guessing.

SUPERFICIAL
AND FALSE INTERPRETATIONS

The fact that understanding rock art is difficult does not mean that it cannot be attempted, nor that reasonably well-founded conclusions cannot be drawn. Unfortunately, two factors have given rock art studies a somewhat questionable status in the minds of many professional scholars. The first is the many premature explanations put forward with great enthusiasm but based on no evidence whatever. There is a tendency to interpret rock art on the basis of what is in the observers' minds rather than what was in the minds of the makers of the art. An extreme example of this is the explanation deriving rock art from the activities of space-men or people from lost continents.

One school of thought is convinced that rock art is writing. Indeed, written inscriptions on rocks do occur in those parts of the world where writing was known, but it remains to be demonstrated that writing is present in most rock art. Writing, by definition, is the representation of the spoken language by some set of symbols, and in this sense the great majority of rock art is not writing. Some people suggest that specific New World rock art sites are written messages left by literate visitors, and the proposed languages include just about every ancient written script: Japanese, Chinese, Babylonian, Egyptian, Greek, and Runic, among others. None of these claims have been taken seriously by experts on the writing systems involved, and the repeated loose claims for "translations" of rock art inscriptions have done little for the credibility of rock art research.

Scholars also have questioned the validity of rock art studies because there is clearly no way of *proving* most of the interpretations. To many scientific researchers, a conclusion that cannot be verified is only speculation and not worth a lot of time and effort. Obviously most rock art was made by people who are now gone, and in many areas there is no living person who has even remnants of the knowledge and viewpoint of the ancient artists. We cannot ask dead people what they were up to, so we must live with the reality that many details of rock art never can be reliably interpreted. There remain, however, several kinds of evidence, and several lines of reasoning, that allow for plausible and often convincing explanations. If we cannot interpret each and every symbol, we *can* often explain the basic motivations which led to the creation of rock art sites. Such explanation can provide insights into the minds of the ancient artists.

ETHNOGRAPHIC
AND HISTORIC
ACCOUNTS

The best and most plausible interpretations come to us from ethnographic and historic accounts in which the nature and purpose of the rock art was actually explained by someone who knew about or participated in the making of rock art (fig. 6-1). There are a few places in the world today, such as Australia, where rock art is still being created and/or renewed, and where rock art still plays an important role in native rituals. Here living people can provide reliable testimony about it. In other areas, while rock art is no longer being produced, there are living people who have been told about the rock art by their parents and grandparents, and in some cases, they may even know who produced the rock art, when, and for what purpose (Conway, n.d; Michaelis, 1981). In a few areas where

6-1 Willow Springs, Arizona, petroglyphs showing clan symbols as recorded enthnographically in the last century and further analyzed by Michaelis (1981). Photo Helen Michaelis, 1976.

161

native cultures still persist, living people have traditional beliefs about rock art and may act on the basis of these beliefs. For reasons of territorial claims, members of one tribe have sometimes obliterated rock art known to be produced by another tribe, in an attempt to eliminate evidence which might be used in a land claims dispute. All of this shows that there is a considerable body of knowledge about rock art among aboriginal peoples. Such direct information is invaluable although it is hard to get and must be evaluated carefully. Most native informants of today are separated by centuries from the creation of the surviving rock art, and they may be as ignorant of the intentions of the artists as you are. Further, natives may deliberately mislead outsiders in order to obscure sacred knowledge. Early missionaries, travelers, and others who inquired about rock art were usually told that it was made by ancient ancestors, or sometimes by a mythical race which formerly existed. The living people claimed to know nothing about it. Sometimes that was true, but often the informant did not want to talk about rock art to outsiders.

The exciting findings of linkages between some rock art and contemporary peoples do not, however, justify the assumption that all the rock art in a given area was produced by the direct ancestors of the tribe that occupied the region in recent times. Much rock art is clearly very ancient and has no relationship to recent peoples. Interpreters must be very careful about referring to rock art as "Hopi," "Chumash," or other tribal designations. Unless the age of the art is known and it can be tied to recent peoples, it is better to define styles using terms which do not have ethnic or tribal connotations. Hence the use of geographic or other terms to define rock art styles, such as the "Giant Mural Style" in Baja California, or the "Great Basin Style" of large areas of deserts in the western United States.

One basis for interpretation is in the basic features of many human groups, past and present, who shared some fundamental belief systems. If the belief system was shamanism, there are some universal features of shamanic belief which can provide insights for many rock art sites and even for individual rock art elements. This is a safe assumption for rock art produced by hunters and gatherers in all parts of the New World.

162

A certain amount of very useful information also comes from recorded folklore and mythology of the native peoples of a region. A rock art site in southern California may have reference to a Chumash myth about a sun-bearer (fig. 6-2). As another example, in much of the western U.S. there is extensive mythology about a pair of "heavenly twins" who were involved in the creation of the earth and many mythical events (fig. 6-3). It is logical (although not *provable*) that the common occurrence of pairs of human figures in the rock art of this region refers to this pair and their exploits. This artistic feature cannot be attributed to accidental association, since such paired human figures are rare everywhere else in North America.

6-2 *Small pictograph which may illustrate a Chumash myth in which the sun is said to be an old man carrying a torch across the sky. The anthropomorphic figure holds a "sun disk" in one hand. Edgar Rock, Carrizo Plain, California. Photo 1981.*

6-3 *Possible portrayal of the "Heavenly Twins," central to much mythology in the western U.S. Gillian County, Oregon. Photo from Loring Collection, UCLA Rock Art Archive.*

INDIRECT
INTERPRETATION

Indirect interpretation depends on finding the motifs or elements of the rock art duplicated in other kinds of artistic representations or items of material culture. This is particularly valuable in linking rock art with *archaeological* remains, providing a suggestion of the age and cultural affiliations of the rock art. In Baja California, a device formerly used by shamans is a *"tabla,"* a broad wand of wood decorated with geometric designs (fig. 6-4). One particular design used on these *tablas* also occurs in the rock art of some sites of this area, and while it is a fairly simple hour-glass element, its occurrence at selected rock art sites indicates that it may well be related to the shamanic beliefs of the late prehistoric period.

Another example is in the archaeology of Chile, where the same "condor man" figure appearing in rock art (fig. 6-5) was found as a figure made of gold (fig. 6-6). In this case, since the gold figure can be dated to about 2,000 years ago, there is a likelihood that the rock art figure is of similar age, and furthermore, that the archaeological culture responsible for the gold figure was also responsible for the rock art. This opens the door to many interpretive possibilities, since the archaeological culture provides much information not present in the rock art. Not only dating information, but also data on the settlements, houses, artifacts, and burial customs of the people who produced the rock art may be recoverable if the art can be linked to the archaeological record.

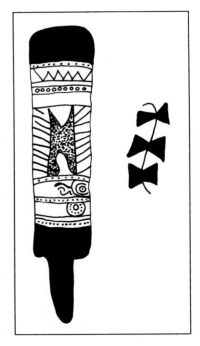

6-4 Left, a wooden "tabla" from a cave in central Baja California. Right, a "butterfly" motif from rock art of the same area, that is similar to the basic element of the tabla.

164

6-5 (left)   Figure of "condor man" in petroglyphs (actual size of the figure about 10 cm. in height). Tamentica, Chile, photo 1969.   6-6 (right) The "condor man" in sheet gold from a site in the same area (note the small wings projecting from the legs). The artifact is dated at about 2,000 years ago; the rock art is presumed to be of similar age because of the identical iconography.

ALTERNATIVE INTERPRETATIONS

A checklist of many meanings which can plausibly be attributed to individual rock art sites is proposed by Meighan (1981: 16). The meanings include 12 general areas of interpretation, and this does not exhaust the possibilities:

• Boundary markers or representations of group symbols having territorial significance.

• Clan or personal symbols representing the "I was here" message (see fig. 6-1).

• Hunting magic: ritual intended to increase the supply of game. This is often depicted in pictures of prey animals with arrows across them (fig. 6-7) or imbedded in them.

6-7 Pictograph showing game animal (deer) crossed by arrow. Pajaro Negro site, Baja California. Photo 1962.

• Supplication, exemplified by cupule rock art (the so-called "rain rocks" or "baby rocks")—marks made by individuals to accompany a prayer or request for some benefit (see fig. 1-29, 1-30, 1-31).

• Astronomical or calendric significance. An increasing number of sites appear to have been produced in connection with solstice observances (fig. 6-8). Some sites have also been interpreted as related to the appearance of comets.

• Initiation rituals including puberty ceremonies, known ethnographically to be the explanation for some rock art. It is plausible to assume that much rock art was used in instructing the young or revealing "mysteries" to initiates (fig. 6-9).

• Representations of mental experiences such as dreams, visions of guardian spirits, mythical beings, phosphenes. These may or may not

166

summer solstice

autumnal equinox

vernal equinox

winter solstice

6-8 *Solstice site at Fajada Butte, New Mexico, showing how daggers of sunlight are linked to the spiral petroglyph at specific seasonal dates. Reproduced by permission from the Griffith Observer 47:6, p. 10. (Drawing by Michael Bieniasz, after Anna Sofaer). For published reference see Zeilik, 1983.*

6-9 *Pictograph site in San Diego County, California, known to have been used in girls' puberty ceremonies. The girls ran a race to the rock and made their mark (zigzag lines or dots) in red or black paint. Photo D. L. True, 1958.*

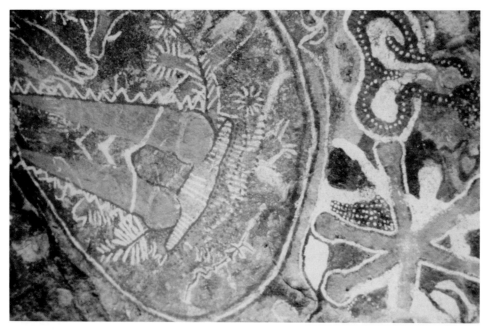

6-10 This multi-colored picture with diverse elements is not a "picture" to our eyes, but certainly represented a complex set of images in the mind of the artist. Pleito Creek, Ventura County, California. Photo Georgia Lee. 1978.

be drug-induced visions, but the rock art would represent some aspect of the mental experience of the artist (fig. 6-10).

• Important historical events, such as wars and battles, coming of outsiders or alien peoples, or spectacular natural events (such as comets). A number of rock art sites in North America show Europeans on horseback, and even such marvels as trains and steamboats. These new experiences were so striking to the native people that they were commemorated in a rock art representation (fig. 6-11). No doubt dramatic events of prehistoric times were also commemorated in this way.

• Witchcraft and magical control over enemies, dangerous animals, or ghosts and spirits.

• Mortuary markers in commemoration of the deceased.

6-11 North American rock art portraying men on horseback, therefore the arrival of Europeans. Canyon de Chelly, Arizona. Photo Frank Bock.

6-12 Contemporary rock art. Tarahumara boy who produced this rock art in 1989, stating that he did it to while away the time while tending animals. The elements produced bear a strong resemblance to Great Basin rock art. Photo Jay Levi, 1989.

• Doodling or more or less random marks done to while away the time; markings which are said by informants to lack any particular significance (fig. 6-12).

• Aesthetics: the deliberate enhancement of special places by adding to them striking and colorful images. This has been compared to the decoration of churches, since sacred art occurs in sacred places, and much rock art is located in exceptional and dramatic locations.

No doubt this list is not inclusive of all possibilities, but it is long enough to provide a major caution in drawing conclusions: not all rock art has the same meaning. It is a first rule of scientific study, in archaeology as in other fields, that **alternative explanations need to be considered for observed phenomena.** This requires thinking about the supporting evidence for all the possible explanations and reaching a conclusion based on the best possible interpretation. Rock art studies will not advance if researchers do not think through all the possibilities and try to reason which is most likely to be true.

SYMBOLISM

One reason why it is unrealistic to expect that we will ever be able to "decode" all rock art is the common use of symbols—elements which carry the same meaning to members of one particular social group, but have no meaning to those who have not learned what the symbols stand for.

Very similar symbols are also found in ancient rock art sites, particularly such simple elements as crosses, which are almost universal. But the message sent and received by such symbols (fig. 6-13) could have no relationship to the meanings these symbols communicate to people in the Western world today: Christianity, the Nazi party, or the peace movement. Whatever meaning may have been present, it must have had some different referent in the context of prehistoric rock art. Frustrating as it is, we may never be able to decipher the particular meaning of many symbols in rock art. Of course, there is historic rock art as well as ancient rock art, and the symbols of recent rock art may well carry the same message we recognize today. Christian crosses, for example, appear as later additions to many ancient rock art sites; in some cases these were added by more recent visitors who wanted to put a Christian symbol with those of pagan artists.

This diversity of meaning among different cultural groups greatly complicates the problem of interpreting symbols because the specific in-

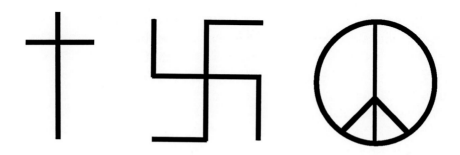

6-13 Symbols which carry variable meaning depending on the viewer, his cultural background, and the time period. Example: "Christian" crosses occur in rock art which is older than the birth of Christ.

terpretation by the viewer is so variable. The Christian cross, for example, might inspire one viewer to reverence or consideration of Christian themes and prayers, while the cross might carry no message at all and be just a mark on the rock to another viewer.

A further complexity is the difficulty of recognizing the symbolic content from pictorial images. A complex geometric figure in South American rock art has been demonstrated to be a diagrammatic representation of a fish trap (Williams, 1985; fig. 6-14). Such drawings are mostly associated with rapids and waterfalls, places where the fish-traps were no doubt effective. But are these merely drawings of fish traps or do they have some symbolic meaning as well—magical ways of insuring a good catch of fish, or perhaps even religious symbols referring to water creatures or water spirits?

6-14. Rock art representations of fish traps (After Williams, 1985)

As with the motivations for creating rock art at all, the creation of the specific kinds of rock art elements has many possible interpretations. Certain things were selected for emphasis and are repeatedly reproduced; these selected elements are often restricted to small geographic regions and particular time periods. Surely they show us something of what was in the minds of the artists. Why draw fish-traps if you are not thinking of fish? The artists who produced such images were not thinking of deer-hunting or comets and were not developing images that we would find elsewhere. Hence, while we may be frustrated at not being able to "read" each and every symbol, we should be pleased to develop some understanding of the *general* meaning of the rock art activity in different times and places. For example, while we may not know the myths, legends, and rituals related to hunting magic in a particular location, if we can recognize the rock art as most likely being related to hunting magic, we know something of importance. We have identified the use of the rock art as belonging to a particular realm of human experience, and have eliminated other, less likely explanations.

DATING ROCK ART

Determining the age of rock art is extremely difficult but some methods exist, and others are being explored and developed, to determine when the rock art was produced. The question of relative dating or sequence has been previously discussed in connection with the recording of superimpositions. Here it is the calendar age of the rock art that is of concern: how many years have elapsed since the rock art was produced? Lacking written inscriptions or dates, how can there be some reliable estimation of age?

172

ELEMENTS IN THE ROCK ART ITSELF

Pictures of extinct animals are an obvious indication of age if you know when the animals became extinct. The best-known examples are the Paleolithic cave paintings of Europe which show mammoth, rhinoceros, and other animals which have not lived in southern Europe for over 12,000 years. In Australia also, there appear to be representations of extinct animals in the rock art.

Cultural objects can also be a general indicator of age. In the Coso rock art area of southern California, there are pictures of spearthrowers (fig. 1-15, 6-15) and pictures of people with bows and arrows (figs. 6-16, 6-17). Since we know the bow and arrow was introduced to the area at about the beginning of the Christian era, there is some basis for deciding that the petroglyphs with spearthrowers are mostly older than this date.

6-15.   *Petroglyphs showing spear-throwers. Coso rock art site, California. Photo 1986.*

*6-16   Petroglyph showing men shooting at one another with bow and arrow.   Little Petroglyph Canyon, Coso
rock art site, California. Photo 1986.*

*6-17   Petroglyph showing man shooting at a mountain sheep with bow and arrow.   Big Petroglyph Canyon,
Coso rock art site, California. Photo 1956.*

174

Petroglyphs showing bows and arrows must be less than 2,000 years old.

And of course, we have the previously mentioned rock art of the historical period, showing such things as conquistadors on horses, Christian churches with crosses, and recent items of material culture such as rifles. The age of such art is easily fixed by reference to the written history of when such items came into the area where the rock art is found.

ASSOCIATIONAL DATES

Most rock art is dated by an *associational date* rather than by a direct date on the art itself. This is much easier to obtain than a direct date on the art, but it is also subject to greater uncertainty. An actual example of an associational date is the radiocarbon dating of a wooden artifact which was found in a Baja California cave, the walls of which are decorated with elaborate rock art. The assumption is made that the same people who lived in the cave and left the artifacts behind are responsible for the art, and that the 600-year age of the artifact also applies to the cave paintings. This is plausible but could be wrong, because the artifacts may have been left by earlier or later inhabitants. A better case can be made for a painted cave in Argentina, where portions of the wall bearing pictographs fell off and were buried in midden refuse accumulated by residents of the cave. By dating charcoal in the layers above and below the painted fragments, it was possible to get a fix on the time period when the rock art fell—in this case several thousand years ago.

Recorders of a rock art site may sometimes be able to collect samples that could be used for associational dating. The best of these are charcoal or other organic material that can be dated by radiocarbon, or obsidian chipping waste which can be dated by obsidian hydration measurements. However, care must be taken in looking for such samples. **You cannot conduct any excavations and must confine yourself to items found on the surface.** These may yield erroneous or misleading results. Obviously, anything found on the surface could have been dropped there at any time. In addition, charcoal or charred firewood may not be ancient, but instead may be left from fires of recent campers. Hence, while the recorders may keep an eye out for suitable dating samples, the context must be carefully observed to avoid any possible confusions. If there is a lot of recent garbage at the site (beverage cans, etc.), it is unlikely that a good dating sample can be found without an excavation program.

RADIOCARBON DATING

Direct determinations of age are obviously the most reliable, and the C-14 (radiocarbon) method of dating organic material would appear to be an easy way of finding out when rock art was made. Researchers have tried to date the paint used to make the rock art, either the charcoal used for black paint or the organic binders used in other mineral pigments. The minute amount of such organic material preserved in rock art has not been sufficient to allow for reliable dating so far. However, the increasing precision and sensitivity of radiocarbon and in particular, the development of dating techniques using linear accelerators, offers promise that some rock art may be directly dated even though very small samples of pigment (on the order of milligrams) can be obtained. This approach shows promise, but it is not applicable to rock art where no organic material is present (e.g. nearly all petroglyphs).

CATION-RATIO DATING

Not useful for painted rock art, but potentially very valuable for dating petroglyphs, are chemical changes in the patination of the rock surface. The cation-ratio method is based on the fact that when the surface is chipped to make rock art, fresh rock is exposed which then proceeds to change chemically (re-patinate) to match the natural surface of the rock (Dorn and Whitley, 1983, 1984; Nobbs and Dorn, 1988). This method, known as cation-ratio dating, is based on the relative proportions of elements in the patina, and the differential loss of some elements to weathering with the passage of time. Preliminary research has been promising and suggests that some rock art in the desert areas of North America (and in Australia) is many thousands of years old. It offers the possibility of determining not only the sequence, but the actual age of many sites which are now impossible to date.

Use of this method requires complex laboratory analyses, and in addition, a determination of the rate at which the chemical changes are proceeding. It has to be calibrated by reference to some rock art which can be dated by other means. In the western U.S., the calibration was developed by doing chemical analyses of rock art of historic age and of older rock art for which there was some dating evidence. The general application of the method is still being developed; it is experimental and will require extensive additional study before it can be applied to new regions. Like other dating methods, cation-ratio dating is not a universal technique which can apply to all rock art everywhere. It works only on petroglyphs which are placed on certain kinds of rock. It can also be used to determine the age of manufacture of certain stone tools.

Because of these new possibilities for dating, it is extremely important not to do anything to the rock art that might contaminate the pigments or change the chemistry of the rock art surfaces in any way.

OTHER DATING METHODS

Several other methods for determining the age of rock art have been explored (see, for example, Weisbrod, 1978; Harrington and Whitney, 1987). Examples include efforts to estimate the time required for observed color changes to take place, for slow-growing lichens to cover the rock art, or for deposition of soil over rock art faces. All of these methods are subject to variables that cannot be controlled. For example, although lichens are very slow-growing, they are plants and their growth can be affected by available water and sunlight, which can vary tremendously even within a single site. Therefore, while often ingenious and plausible, such dating methods are unproven in determining "years ago" ages for rock art. They are primarily useful in relative dating—suggesting which are the older and newer elements—particularly if applied to only a single site with uniform environmental conditions.

While determinations of the "years ago" ages of rock art are still in their infancy, it is easy to see that when the problem of accurate dating is resolved, a whole new era of rock art studies will be launched. When the sites can be arranged in time, and hence related to other kinds of archaeological evidence, rock art will become a much more valuable part of the archaeological and prehistoric record. Furthermore, the ability to recognize the time span during which a site was used will also allow us to see changes in the style of rock art internally, within the same site. Accurate determination of the age of rock art is probably the single most important advance that can be made in rock art studies, and it is encouraging that an increasing number of scholars are taking on the challenge of determining rock art chronology.

Unfortunately, technical dating studies are not something most rock art recorders can do, since they will not have the training or the laboratory facilities needed. However, recorders *can* often contribute to chronological information. Their notes and observations can identify rock art sites which have the potential for dating (from associated archaeological material that can be excavated). The rock art recorder can also provide essential information about *relative* age by recording superimpositions carefully and making observations of color changes and other indications that appear to separate newer from older rock art at their site. The recorders task is to think about chronology and not merely assume that everything in his site is of the same age.

Since dating procedures which require laboratory facilities also require controlled samples collected and recorded in a specific way, field recorders need a contact with the dating laboratory to know what kind of sample is useful and how it should be collected. For potential radiocarbon dates, there are numerous laboratories, some attached to universities and some commercial laboratories which will test any sample for a fee. For more experimental methods (or even new ones you might think up yourself), there are fewer people who can help, but available contacts may be identifiable through a call to your local university or to the established rock art societies.

The determination of the age of rock art is one of the most critical problems which must be solved if we are to relate rock art to other aspects of the historical and archaeological record. We need to know how many years have gone by since the artists produced their work, and we also need to know how long a given rock art location was in use. While it is frustrating to recognize that much rock art cannot be dated with the techniques currently available, significant advances have been made in recent years, and it is likely that new methods of dating will be developed in the near future.

7

SAFEGUARDING THE RECORD

Those who have followed all the suggestions for recording a rock art site so far, will have accumulated a praiseworthy collection of notes, drawings, photographs, and other data. They have gained a great deal of knowledge, and perhaps some understanding as well, of the rock art at "their" site. In fact, they may have become the world's expert on their particular rock art site—not a small accomplishment.

To safeguard the records resulting from all this effort is an important final task. A site found and not reported is lost once again. A set of notes and records which is destroyed by fire, flood, or other catastrophe leaves all of the work to be done once more. There are many known cases in which the original field notes disappeared through misadventures, such as insect or rodent damage, decomposition of the paper, stolen luggage, or even confiscation by customs officials. The list is a long one and the losses are always unexpected and painful.

The making of an insurance copy is an easy task that should not be overlooked. Some field workers, particularly those who have lost records previously, are so conscious of this problem that they make carbon copies of all documents in the field. When in the field for an extended period of time, they put the carbon copies in an envelope and mail them home just to be sure that the records will survive if the originals are "lost in transit."

Should you be fortunate enough to have several helpers in the field recording the same site, you, as crew chief, should insist that copies of every record be made and turned in promptly, preferably while you are still in the field. That way, you can assure there is one comprehensive master set of records and not merely a lot of individual notes scattered among a number of recorders. If the comprehensive notes are not assembled as soon as possible, there is a high risk that some key part of the documentation will be found missing when the overall report is finally prepared.

CENTRAL RECORD FILES AND ARCHIVES

Aside from the problem of potential loss, existence of a single copy of the records will be of little value if you are the only one who knows of these documents. Records kept at home tend to get buried deeper and deeper in household accumulations. Field notes which were very exciting at the time of the recording, wind up on the shelf, then in the attic, then in the garage, and when you are gone these documents may well get thrown away if they have no meaning for your heirs. You can therefore kill two birds with one stone by filing the copy of your records with an appropriate institution. This gets the insurance copy safely filed apart from the original, and it also serves to make your records a part of a larger data base, likely to be consulted by others seeking information about your site. This will provide a dated documentation effort of immense value to future workers, and at best it may save a great deal of redundant effort as people unwittingly retrace your steps and re-do all of your work. Of course, it is better that they take up where you left off rather than repeat records you have already compiled.

Whether or not you are able to submit a full descriptive report, it is strongly recommended that a *site record form* (discussed in Chapter 2; sample forms in Appendix A) be filed with your local university, museum, or State Historic Preservation Office. This will place the site in the official records and will insure that its location and the basic features of the rock art are known. Eventually it will assure that these facts are entered into one of the many computerized data banks being developed nationwide. While this is an essential first step, it should be noted that most of the agencies maintaining records of archaeological remains do not treat rock art sites separately from other site records, and your record form will become one of many thousands for your state.

If you become an aficionado and develop a whole report on a given site, you should file your copy with a specialized repository that deals specifically with rock art and maintains detailed records on rock art sites. There are few such facilities, but most countries have at least one institution that maintains detailed records on rock art sites and has a reasonably comprehensive set of files on such sites. In the United States, the institutionally based facility of this kind is the **Rock Art Archive, Institute of Archaeology, University of California, Los Angeles 90024 (Phone 213-825-1720).** This office has thousands of files of original documentation of rock art sites. It serves as a research facility as well as a repository for rock art records.

Most workers are justifiably reluctant to give up copies of the work on which they have spent time, effort, and also money, since they do not want their efforts exploited by others. However, the individual workers can expect that their records will be cited and that they will be given credit and recognition for the notes and photographs they have contributed. Any responsible repository will insist that all photographs and records that are used in publication will provide credit lines indicating who collected the original data. There need not be anxiety that one's records will be "stolen" if they are made part of the general body of scientific knowledge. It is more likely that field documentation will be filed away in an archive and not studied in detail for many years, until someone comes along who is looking for exactly the kind of information you have collected. At that time, you may be gone and the site may be gone, but your efforts will be both recognized and appreciated by scholars who are consulting your irreplaceable documentation.

A few rock art recorders have become so involved with their subject that they develop published reports and even write books on their sites and findings. For those with this much time and energy, advice and help can be found in the universities and scholarly organizations with rock art specialists. Most recorders prefer to leave the final scholarly analysis to those who have the time and the training to use the data and carry it to the next step. To go beyond a description of the site: to interpret, determine the age, and provide comparative analysis of regional rock art, is a task demanding a tremendous amount of time and effort. It is well within the capabilities of a recorder to undertake these additional tasks, but it is beyond the scope of this manual to consider them in detail. The first step is to discover a rock art site that has never been well documented and then to record it to the best of your ability. That is a satisfying accomplishment in itself.

CONSERVATION OF ROCK ART

Not only is it important that your records be preserved, but of course it is very important that the site of the rock art be preserved as well. You can make an important contribution by calling your site to the attention of those whose job it is to conserve cultural resources. You may be aware of actual or potential damage to your site and may be able to arouse local or institutional interest in preserving the rock art. If the site you are recording appears to be in imminent danger of destruction, it is important to call the site to the attention of your State Historic Preservation Office which may instigate whatever "management" procedures are needed, including the possibility of intensive emergency studies. Lee (in press) provides some guidelines for cultural resource management as it pertains to rock art. See also American Rock Art Research Association, 1988.

Efforts to preserve rock art are also worth mention since they will inevitably entail physical modifications. Rock art recorders who have examined their sites carefully enough to look at all the individual elements will recognize places where the rock art is deteriorating due to wind, water, or whatever. Recorders will rarely be directly involved with preservation or conservation procedures, but they need to know enough about them to realize that this is also a task for experts.

Many poorly-thought-out efforts to preserve rock art have had the opposite effect. For example, building shelters or putting glass panels over the art may cause moisture to be trapped in the rock so that the whole surface spalls off. The site of Nanaimo in British Columbia is an example of a location where a shelter built to protect the rock art caused moisture to be trapped, and the shelter had to be removed. The placing of panels over the rock art also changes the effects of moisture and may trap leaves and organic material against the rock art as well. In Japan, a rock art site was enclosed in a museum building to protect it, but the change in humidity inside the building caused development of a mold on the petroglyphs.

There have also been some poorly though out attempts to stabilize rock surfaces by impregnating the rock with some chemical, but in some cases these have actually hastened deterioration and caused the rock art to spall off in big sections. The method is valid, but the application of it requires specialized knowledge and skill. Hence, physical or chemical actions to preserve the rock art should not be attempted by recorders. All the recorder can do is make careful note of the conditions leading to deterioration of the site. The recorder may also know enough, from what is said here, to act as a voice of caution to local enthusiasts who want to launch into well-meaning but ill-advised "preservation" activities.

Recent years have seen considerable attention devoted to conservation of rock art sites (see for example Crotty, 1989; Lambert, 1988). Some ingenious techniques have been developed, including the placing of a ribbon of silicon sealant around a rock art panel to direct rain or seepage around the rock art and prevent water from flowing over it. There have also been a few successful efforts to restore rock art sites which have been damaged by vandalism. Restoration of a damaged site is a far more complex task than mere protection of the rock art, since it often involves the removal of spray paint, filling in bullet holes, and similar actions requiring extensive knowledge of chemistry and the nature of the rock surfaces. The Getty Research Institute in Los Angeles regularly offers training programs in conservation of rock art and is actively developing new methods.

THE RECORD AS
A VALUABLE HISTORIC DOCUMENT

We end this book on the same note which began it: the value of documenting rock art when and where we find it. While the conservation of sites and rock art is important, all too many rock art sites exist today *only* in the form of the photographs and drawings made by a recorder. The site is gone and no one in the future will be able to make further study of it. Those of us who have had the pleasure of discovering and recording rock art locations over the years can also recount what has become of the sites we recorded in the past—too many of them are under the waters of a reservoir or obliterated by vandalism, including not only spray paint and chiselled initials, but bullets, dynamite, and deliberate destruction with bulldozers. Many others are removed in the process of building roads, airports, and subdivisions. We cannot assume that any rock art, no matter how remote and "protected" it appears, will be there next year.

The fascination of finding and documenting rock art is rewarding in itself, but it is also useful because it preserves many evidences of ancient humanity that would otherwise vanish. Rock art is one of the few tangible evidences that show us directly what was in the minds of people in the past. It records some chapters in the history of the human race that are not recorded in any other way, and for this reason alone it is worthy of our study and appreciation.

187

# REFERENCES

This list of references is divided into two parts: general works, and regional studies which describe the rock art of delimited areas. Many of the latter also include comments and suggestions on methods of recording appropriate for the needs of each region's rock art. Although general works are listed, this is not intended to be a comprehensive bibliography on rock art studies. It includes those articles which are used as examples for points discussed in the text. In addition to the works cited, there are a number of journals and symposium volumes which appear regularly. The American Rock Art Research Association publishes *American Indian Rock Art,* papers from their annual conference (Volumes 1-11, 1975-1984, are available). The San Diego Museum of Man also publishes annual rock art symposium volumes (Volumes 1-6, 1982-1989) are available.

GENERAL PUBLICATIONS AND METHODOLOGY

American Rock Art Research Association
    1988   Conservation Guidelines of the American Rock Art Research Association. San Miguel, California.

Anati E.
    1977   Methods of recording and analyzing rock art engravings. Studi Camuni Edizioni del Dentro, Brescia.

Apostolides, Alex
    1975   Recording rock art. *The Artifact,* 13(1): 30-35. El Paso Archaeological Society, El Paso.

Bahn, Paul G.
    1989   *Images of the Ice Age.* Facts on File, New York.

Bain, James G.
1975   *Techniques and procedures for rock art recording.* Mono-
            graph 3, Coos Publishing and Research, Las Cruces.

Breschini, Gary and Trudy Haversat
1983   *La Cueva Pintada: A technical report on documenting the*
            rock paintings at National Register Site CA-Mnt-256 (4
            vols.). Coyote Press, Salinas.

Clewlow, C. William and Mary Ellen Wheeling
1978   *Rock art: An introductory recording manual for*
            California and the Great Basin. Institute of Archaeology,
            University of California, Los Angeles.

Conway, Thor
n.d.   Ojibway oral history relating to 19th Century Rock Art.
            Paper presented at American Rock Art
            Research Association meeting, Ridgecrest [1988].

Crotty, Helen K.
1981   Petroglyph Point Revisited—A Modoc County Site. In:
            Messages from the Past (C. Meighan, ed.), Institute of Ar-
            chaeology, University of California, Monograph XX, pp.
            141-168. Los Angeles.

Crotty, Helen K., editor
1989   Preserving our Rock Art Heritage. *American Rock Art Re-*
            search Association, Occasional Paper 1, San Miguel, Cali-
            fornia.

Day, Jane S., ed.
1989   Rock art of the Western Canyons. *Denver Museum of Natu-*
            ral History/Colorado Archaeological Society Memoir 3.
            Denver.

DeKorne, James B.
1973   How to photograph rock art. *El Palacio,* 77(1): 14-17.
            Santa Fe.

Dorn, Ronald I. and David S. Whitley
1983   Cation-ratio dating of petroglyphs from the
            Western Great Basin, North America. *Nature,* 302 (5911):
            816-818. London.

190

| | 1984 | Chronometric and relative age determinations of petro-glyphs in the Western United States. *Annals of the Association of American Geographers* 74:2, 318-322. |

Dubelaar, C. N.
1981   The Distribution of Im Thurn's Elaborate Type petroglyphs in South America. *Compte-rendu des Communications du Congrès International d'Études des Civilisations Précolombiennes des Petites Antilles,* 9:375-97. Montreal.

1986a   An inventory of the petroglyphs in the Guianas and adjacent areas of Brazil and Venezuela, with a comprehensive bibliography of South American and Antillean petroglyphs. University of California Institute of Archaeology, *Monumenta Archaeologica,* 12. Los Angeles.

1986b   *South American and Caribbean petroglyphs.* Foris Publications. Dordrecht, Holland/ Riverton, U.S.A.

Fenenga, Franklin
1949   Methods of recording and present status concerning petroglyphs of California. *University of California Archaeological Survey Reports* 3: 1-19. Berkeley.

Grant, Campbell
1967   *Rock art of the American Indian.* T. Y. Crowell Co., New York.

Green, John W.
1976   The study of early photographs of rock art sites to enhance the accuracy of later investigations. *American Indian Rock Art,* 11: 66-82. El Paso.

Harrington, Charles D. and John W. Whitney
1987   Scanning electron microscope method for rock-varnish dating. *Geology* 15:967-970.

Hyder, William D. and Mark Oliver
1983   The 35mm camera and rock art photography. In: *Ancient Images on Stone* (JoAnne Van Tilburg, ed.): 96-101. Institute of Archaeology, University of California, Los Angeles.

Krupp, E.C.
    1983   Light and Shadow. *Griffith Observer* 47:6, 12-20. Griffith Observatory, Los Angeles.

Lambert, David   *Conserving Australian Rock Art, A Manual for*
    1988   *Site Managers.* Aboriginal Studies Press, Canberra.

Lee, Georgia
    in press   Rock art and cultural resource management. Wormwood Press, Calabasas, Calif.

Loendorf, Lawrence, Linda Olsen, and Stuart Conner
    1988   A Recording Manual for Rock Art. Ms. prepared during research at the Piñon Canyon Maneuver Site. University of North Dakota.

Mallery, Garrick
    1893   Picture-Writing of the American Indians. *Tenth Annual Report of the Bureau of American Ethnology:* 1-822. Washington.
    1896   Pictographs of the North American Indians. *Fourth Annual Report of the Bureau of American Ethnology:* 3-256. Washington.

Meighan, Clement W.
    1981   Theory and practice in the study of rock art. In: *Messages from the Past* (C. W. Meighan, ed.): 3-20. Monograph 20, Institute of Archaeology, University of California, Los Angeles.

Michaelis, Helen
    1981   Willowsprings: A Hopi Petroglyph Site. *Journal of New World Archaeology:* 4:2, 3-23. University of California, Los Angeles.

Nobbs, Margaret F. and Ronald I. Dorn
    1988   Age Determinations for Rock Varnish Formation within Petroglyphs: Cation-ratio dating of 24 motifs from the Olary Region, South Australia. *Rock Art Research* 5:2, 108-146. Australian Rock Art Research Association, Melbourne.

Pohorecky, Zenon S. and T. E. H. Jones
    1966   Recording rock paintings. *Man* 2:2, 305-306.
    1967   Recording pictographs. *Man* 1:1, 104.

Saenz, Karen, Bill Joyner and Robert Morrow
    in press   Montage photography of Rock Art. Ms. to be
                  published in Rock Art Research and La Pintura.
                  [1988]

Schaafsma, Polly
    1981   Kachinas in Rock Art. *Journal of New World Archaeology*,
                  4:2, 24-32. University of California, Los Angeles.

Schaafsma, Polly, and Curtis F. Schaafsma
    1974   Evidence for the Origins of the Pueblo Katchina Cult as
                  Suggested by Southwestern Rock Art.
                  American Antiquity 39: 535-545. Washington.

Steinbring, Jack and Franklin Farvour
    1987   The Hensler Petroglyph Site, Dodge County, Wisconsin.
                  The Wisconsin Archaeologist, 68:4, 396-411. Milwaukee.

Van Rijssen, W. J. J.
    1987   Painting in peril. *The South African Archaeological Bulle-
                  tin* 42: 5-9.

Weisbrod, R.
    1978   Dating technique proposed for petroglyphs. *Science News*,
                  11:4.
Wellmann, Klaus
    1979   *A survey of North American Indian Rock Art*. Akademische
                  Druck u. Verlagsanstalt, Graz.

Whitley, David S. and Ronald I. Dorn
    1987   Rock art chronology in Eastern California. *World
                  Archaeology*, 19: 2, 150-164.
    1988   Cation-ratio Dating of Petroglyphs using PIXE.
                  *Nuclear Instruments and Methods in Physics Re
                  search* B35: 410-414. North/Holland, Amsterdam.

Williams, Denis
    1979   Preceramic Fishtraps on the Upper Essequibo: Report on a Survey of unusual Petroglyphs on the Upper Essequibo and Kassikaityu Rivers 12-28 March 1979. Journal of the Walter Roth Museum of Archaeology and Anthropology, 2:2, 125-140. Georgetown.

    1985   Petroglyphs in the Prehistory of Northern Amazonia and the Antilles. *Advances in World Archaeology* 4:335-387. Academic Press, Orlando.

Zeilik, Michael
    1983   The Sunwatchers of Chaco Canyon. *Griffith Observer*, 47:6, 2-12. Griffith Observatory, Los Angeles.

REGIONAL SUMMARIES AND SURVEYS IN NORTH AMERICA

This section does not attempt to list all articles on various regions, and it is restricted to North America, although there are extensive regional summaries for other areas of the world. The works of Grant, Mallery, and Wellmann (cited above) provide general summaries for North America as a whole. Wellmann, 1979, is a good beginning point because of its extensive illustration of most North American styles, plus a bibliography with over 1,000 references.

The following list includes summaries of the rock art of states and sub-regions in North America:

ALASKA

Emmons, George T.
    1908   Petroglyphs in Southeastern Alaska. *American Anthropologist* 10: 221-230.

ARIZONA

Grant, Campbell
    1978   *Canyon de Chelly: Its people and rock art.* University of Arizona, Tucson.

Schaafsma, Polly
    1980   *Indian rock art of the Southwest.* School of American Research, University of New Mexico, Albuquerque.

Turner, Christy G.
    1963   Petrographs of the Glen Canyon Region. *Museum of Northern Arizona Bulletin* 38. Northern Arizona Society of Science and Art, Flagstaff.

BAJA CALIFORNIA

Crosby, Harry W.
    1984   *The cave paintings of Baja California.* Copley Books, La Jolla.

Grant, Campbell
    1974   *Rock art of Baja California.* Dawson's Book Shop, Los Angeles.

Meighan, Clement W.
    1966   Prehistoric rock paintings in Baja California. *American Antiquity* 31: 372-392. Salt Lake City.
    1969   *Indian art and history: The testimony of prehispanic rock paintings in Baja California.* Dawson's Book Shop, Los Angeles.

BRITISH COLUMBIA

Conner, John
    1968   *Pictographs in the interior of British Columbia.* Wayside, Vernon, British Columbia.

Lundy, Doris M.
    1974   The rock art of the Northwest Coast. Master's thesis, Simon Fraser University, Vancouver.

CALIFORNIA

Grant, Campbell
    1965   *The rock paintings of the Chumash: A study of a California Indian Culture.* University of California Press, Berkeley.

Grant, Campbell, James W. Baird, and J. Kenneth Pringle
    1968   *Rock drawings of the Coso Range.* Maturango Museum, China Lake, Calif.

Harner, M. J.
    1953   Gravel pictographs of the lower Colorado River region. *University of California Archaeological Survey Reports* 20: 1-29. Berkeley.

Hedges, Ken
    1973   Rock Art in Southern California. *Pacific Coast Archaeological Society Quarterly* 9(4): 1-28.

Heizer, Robert F. and C. W. Clewlow, Jr.
    1973   *Prehistoric rock art of California.* Ballena Press, Ramona, Calif. (2 vols.)

Hyder, William D.
    1989   Rock art and Archaeology in Santa Barbara County, California. *San Luis Obispo County Archaeological Society, Occasional Paper No. 13.* San Luis Obispo.

King, Linda Barbey
    1981   The Incised Petroglyph Sites at Agua Dulce, Los Angeles County, California. In: *Messages from the Past* (C. Meighan, ed.), 21-50. Monograph 20, Institute of Archaeology, University of California, Los Angeles.

Lee, Georgia
    1984   Rock art of the Sierra Madre ridge. In: Papers on Chumash rock art, *San Luis Obispo County Archaeological Society, Occasional Paper* 12: 11-46. San Luis Obispo.

Payen, Louis A.
    1959   Petroglyphs of Sacramento and adjoining counties, Calif. *University of California Archaeological Survey Reports* 48: 66-83. Berkeley.

Smith, Gerald A. and Wilson G. Turner
    1975   *Indian rock art of Southern California.* San Bernardino County Museum Association, Redlands.

Steward, Julian H.
    1929   Petroglyphs of California and adjoining states. *University of California Publications in American Archaeology and Ethnology* 24: 47-238. Berkeley.

Van Tilburg, JoAnne, Frank Bock, and A. J. Bock
    1987   The Church Rock Petroglyph Site: Field Documentation and Preliminary Analysis. Redding Museum and Art Center, *Occasional Papers* 4. Redding, California.

Von Werlhof, Jay
    1987   *Spirits of the Earth: A Study of Earthen Art in the North American Deserts. Vol. 1, the Northern Desert.* Imperial Valley College Museum Society, El Centro.

COLORADO

McKern, W. C.
    1928   *Western Colorado petroglyphs.* Bureau of Land Management, Colorado State Office, Denver.

NEVADA

Heizer, Robert F. and Martin A. Baumhoff
    1962   *Prehistoric rock art of Nevada and Eastern California.* University of California Press, Berkeley.

NEW MEXICO

Rohn, Arthur H.
    1989   *Rock Art of Bandelier National Monument.* University of New Mexico Press, Albuquerque.

Schaafsma, Polly
    1975   *Rock Art in New Mexico.* University of New Mexico Press, Albuquerque.

Young, M. Jane
    1988   *Signs from the Ancestors, Zuni Cultural Symbolism and Perceptions of Rock Art.* University of New Mexico Press, Albuquerque.

OHIO

Swauger, James L.
    1984   *Petroglyphs of Ohio.* Ohio University Press, Athens.

OREGON

Cressman, Luther F.
    1937   *Petroglyphs of Oregon.* University of Oregon, Eugene.

Loring, J. Malcolm and Louise Loring
    1982   *Pictographs and petroglyphs of the Oregon country, Part I: Columbia River and Northern Oregon.* Institute of Archaeology, University of California, Los Angeles.
    1983   *Pictographs and petroglyphs of the Oregon country, Part II: Southern Oregon.* Institute of Archaeology, University of California, Los Angeles.

SOUTH DAKOTA

Keyser, James D. and Linea Sundstrom
    1984   Rock art of Western South Dakota: The North Cave Hills and the Southern Black Hills. *Special Publications of the South Dakota Archaeological Society* 9, Sioux Falls.

TENNESSEE

Faulkner, Charles H.
    1986   *The prehistoric native American art of Mud Glyph Cave.* University of Tennessee, Knoxville.

TEXAS

Kirkland, Forrest and W. W. Newcomb, Jr.
    1967   *The rock art of the Texas Indians.* University of Texas, Austin.

Gebhard, David S.
    1960   Prehistoric paintings of the Diablo Region of Western Texas. *Roswell Museum and Art Center Publications in Art and Science* 3, Roswell, New Mexico.
    1965   *Prehistoric rock paintings of the Seminole Canyon area, Val Verde County, Texas.* University of California, Santa Barbara.

UTAH

Castleton, Kenneth B.
　　1978　　　*Petroglyphs and pictographs of Utah* (Vol. I). Utah
　　　　　　　Museum of Natural History, Salt Lake City.
　　1979　　　*Petroglyphs and pictographs of Utah* (Vol. II).
　　　　　　　Utah Museum of Natural History, Salt Lake City.

Schaafsma, Polly
　　1971　　　The rock art of Utah: A study from the Donald Scott Col-
　　　　　　　lection. *Papers of the Peabody Museum, Harvard Univer-*
　　　　　　　sity 65. Cambridge.

WASHINGTON

Hill, Beth and Ray Hill
　　1974　　　*Indian petroglyphs of the Pacific Northwest.* Hancock
　　　　　　　House, Saanichton, British Columbia.

Loring, J. Malcolm and Louise Loring
　　1982　　　(see listing under Oregon)

Meade, Edward
　　1971　　　*Indian rock carvings of the Pacific Northwest.*
　　　　　　　Gray's, Sidney, British Columbia.

WYOMING

Gebhard, David S.
　　1969　　　*The rock art of Dinwoody, Wyoming.* University of Califor-
　　　　　　　nia Art Galleries, Santa Barbara.

 # ACKNOWLEDGMENTS

This work has been much aided by several members of the American Rock Art Research Association who have participated together over a period of years in various meetings, field trips, informal discussions, and exchanges of ideas. Some of our approaches and recommendations are subject to scholarly disagreement and the reviewers of our manuscript are not in agreement with us (or each other) on every statement made in this book. The authors take full responsibility for the viewpoints expressed. At the same time, we gratefully acknowledge the discussion, debate, and practical advice we have received from our collaborators from ARARA, including: A. J. Bock, Frank Bock, Helen Crotty, Jay Crotty, Ken Hedges, Bill Hyder, Georgia Lee, Daniel McCarthy, Helen Michaelis, Esther Schwartz, Jack Schwartz, and JoAnne Van Tilburg. All of these received copies of an early version of this manuscript, and in the course of offering valuable suggestions for improvement, they consulted with many others and passed on to us a multitude of suggestions, so our general thanks must be extended to include a large part of the ARARA membership. In addition, we thank Ed Krupp of the Griffith Observatory and James L. Swauger of the Carnegie Museum for numerous valuable discussions.

Several rock art scholars have generously allowed us to use their photographs and illustrations. Illustrations not credited to others are by the authors. The UCLA Rock Art Archive has originals and/or copies of nearly all the illustrations used in this book. These have been contributed by the recorders acknowledged in the illustration captions. The cover photograph is by Sandra Uchitel.

Countless hours of editorial effort by Joan Seibert saw this book through to completion—it would not have seen the light of day except for her enthusiasm and patience.

GLOSSARY

ABRASION	Rubbing; in rock art, some pictures are produce by using a rock (sometimes with sand) to make grooved lines in the rock. This is not a common rock art technique.
ABSTRACT	Non-representational; geometric or other forms not recognizable as a picture of something. Some ABSTRACT pictures may well turn out to be representations or symbols of NATURALISTIC objects, such as the crescentic horns of the mountain sheep being used to represent that animal without drawing the whole animal. However, the crescent itself is an ABSTRACT figure, not a representational one.
ALIGNMENTS	In rock art, the production of patterns by arranging rocks on the ground surface. These are most often lines or circles, but representational elements are sometimes produced with ALIGNMENTS. The technique may also be used to enhance INTAGLIOS.
AMORPHOUS	Without definable shape, having no particular form.
ANTHROPOMORPH	Human-like form.

ATLATL — Spearthrower or throwing stick: device which extends the arm of the person using the weapon. Commonly shown in some rock art (Australia and Coso Range of California), either alone or in the hands of the hunter.

BASE LINE — Reference line from which maps are drawn.

BEDROCK MORTAR — Bowl-shaped depression in boulders or rock outcrops, used for grinding food materials (generally plant foods) with a pestle. May occur with rock art or be incorporated into rock art. See CUPULE.

CATION-RATIO DATING — Determining the age of rock art (or artifacts) by reference to the chemistry of the patination that has formed since the art was done (or the artifact was made). See PATINA.

CHALK FIGURES — A kind of GEOGLYPH made by removing the overlying soil to expose the underlying rock. Well-known in England.

CUP AND RING — See CUPULES

CUPULES — Small circular depressions in rock surfaces, sometimes occurring in lines or patterns. If large, can be confused with BEDROCK MORTARS. However, bedrock mortars were not made on steep sloping or vertical surfaces, are generally much larger, and usually show polish or wear resulting from use. There are exceptions, but as a rule of thumb, cupules are less than 5 cm. in diameter and less than 3 cm. deep. They may be combined with radiating lines, surrounded by petroglyph circles (CUP AND RING), or connected by grooves.

DESERT VARNISH — The patinated surface of rocks exposed to desert sun for long periods. Generally brown to black in color. The accumulation and depletion of different chemicals in desert varnish can be used for dating rock art since there is a fresh (unpatinated) exposure when the rock art is made and the desert varnish forms again over time. See CATION-RATIO DATING.

ELEMENT

In rock art, any individually defined figure in a site. ELEMENTS are often found in groups called PANELS; these may be individual boulders or natural planes of the rock. If several ELEMENTS are related and probably made at the same time (such as a man shooting at a deer with a bow and arrow, or a line of footprints or other repetitive ELEMENTS), they may be referred to as a SCENE. Not all ELEMENTS are grouped—many are made individually. Not all PANELS have SCENES— many are only collections of individual ELEMENTS.

EXFOLIATION

The flaking away of surface rock, a major problem for some rock art sites where the rock art was made on weathered rock. EXFOLIATION can be rapid where there is fractured rock containing cracks, due to water action or freezing and thawing. It may also be very rapid with layered rocks such as slate or some sandstones.

FRIABLE

Soft and crumbly. Soft sandstone is a good example. It's a poor surface for rock art since it is readily weathered away by wind or water.

GEOGLYPH

Generic term for figures made on the surface of the ground. These include ALIGNMENTS, INTAGLIOS, and CHALK FIGURES. They are often very large; the famous "Nazca lines" are GEOGLYPHS.

GEOMETRIC

Style characterized by designs formed of geometric figures (lines, circles, triangles, squares, etc.). In rock art, used for non-representational elements, although it is possible for representational elements to be made in a geometric style (human figures with triangle bodies, for example).

GROOVE

Linear indentation in a rock surface, usually made by rubbing or incising. Many grooved lines are not rock art, but result from the sharpening of stone or bone implements.

HISTORIC

The period of time which is recorded in written

history. The historic period goes back thousands of years in some parts of the world, but only a century or two in areas where there was no written language until recent explorations.

INCISED

Technique of producing sharp-edged, narrow grooved lines by cutting with a pointed tool. Incising is mostly used on artifacts rather than rock art although some incised rock art styles exist and incising is sometimes used to outline figures or put details in the rock art.

INTAGLIO

A recessed figure. In rock art, applies primarily to ground figures produced by scraping away rocky surfaces to show the underlying soil. See GEO-GLYPH.

MIDDEN

The trash remains of a village. Many archaeological middens are the residential area of a former village and include house-remains, graves, and all the evidences found in an archaeological site. In some areas, middens are separate from the residential area, but for most hunter-gatherer locations, the MIDDEN and the SITE are the same area.

MOTIF

A stylistic element which is characteristic of a given STYLE. Some workers prefer to use MOTIF in place of ELEMENT, but in the usage here, MOTIF carries some meaning in the STYLE of a given rock art assemblage, whereas ELEMENT is a purely descriptive term which can apply to lines, dots, and similar universal things in a rock art assemblage.

MUNSELL COLORS

A standard color reference, reproduced in the Munsell Color Charts. For rock art recording, it is the Munsell Soil Color book which is useful, since most rocks and rock art pigments have soil colors. [Munsell makes color charts for other colors as well, but their expense is not warranted for archaeology or rock art studies].

NATURALISTIC

Realistic or representational, as contrasted with ABSTRACT.

206

NON-REPRESENTATIONAL	Design elements which do not appear to be pictures of anything; mostly geometric figures. Some elements seen by contemporary recorders as non-representational may, in fact, have been clearly recognizable pictures to the makers of the rock art. For example, in South America there are some complex "geometrical" elements now recognized as representations of fish traps. Elements which may appear non-representational (or non-pictorial) to modern recorders can sometimes be moved to the "representational" category as their meaning is recognized.
PANEL	A group of elements in a defined space. Many rock art panels are natural planes or surfaces of the rock which are physically marked off from other areas of the site. Some panels are assemblages of rock art elements separated from other similar rock art by a gap where no other rock art occurs (for example, at both ends of a rock shelter with no rock art in between).
PATINA	In rock art, alteration of rock surfaces due to chemical or other weathering phenomena. It is usually visible as a color change to darker rock surfaces. PATINA will very often be present on the natural rock of a site and the primitive artists produced high-contrast petroglyphs by chipping through the patinated surface so that the lighter underlying layers are visible. PATINA may also be present as weathering in the grooves of the rock art itself, with more ancient elements showing darker color as the patination proceeds. This is the basis of CATION-RATIO DATING. PATINA may be highly visible and concentrated in one area (as in places where there is a seep of water over part of the site). PATINA may also be invisible to the naked eye even though the surface layers are chemically different from those underneath (one reason for caution in making any physical impact on rock art).
PECKING	Technique of producing most petroglyphs, done by striking the rock with a hammerstone to create

multiple small indentations. On most rocks, this is a tapping process rather than a hammering process. Extensive and repeated use of PECKING can produce deep grooves or low-relief figures. (This is the same process used to shape ground-stone artifacts such as axes or pestles).

PETROGLYPH

Art that is pecked, carved, abraded or scratched into a rock surface. PETROGLYPH has been used as a generic term for all rock art by some writers, but contemporary usage discriminates this form of rock art from PICTOGRAPH below. Note that occasionally both rock art techniques are combined at sites that have painted petroglyphs.

PICTOGRAPH

Art that is painted on a rock surface.

PIT AND GROOVE

A kind of rock art which consists of cupules and grooves. See CUPULE

PREHISTORIC

Before the advent of written records. The PREHISTORIC may end thousands of years ago in some places and only a century or two ago in places where written records were unknown until recently.

QUADRUPED

Four-legged creature. A neutral term for defining rock art animals which are done too simply to merit identification as specific creatures (dog, bear, etc.)

RECTILINEAR

Straight lines or groups of lines.

REPRESENTATIONAL

Refers to pictorial and recognizable elements—pictures of animals, humans, birds, arrows, etc. REPRESENTATIONAL rock art is generally easier to define and interpret than NON-REPRESENTATIONAL styles. Note, however, that the art may be REPRESENTATIONAL and yet not easily identifiable. For example, very simple representations might be seen by a recorder as frogs, lizards, or humans, with each interpretation equally possible.

ROCK ALIGNMENT	Design formed on the ground by arranging rocks or boulders to create a pattern. A form of GEO-GLYPH which requires no alteration of the surface, merely the arrangement of rocks. Most rock alignments are linear although circles and other forms occur
ROCK ART	In this book, includes CUPULES, PETRO-GLYPHS, PICTOGRAPHS, and GEOGLYPHS. Excluded from rock art are murals on constructed buildings, sculptures such as stelae or statues, and engraved or painted small artifacts.
SCENE	In rock art, applies to a series of figures which were all produced at the same time and presumably have some relationship to one another as an artistic effort. Example: A group of hunters pursuing a band of animals. SCENES are often (but not always) coterminous with PANELS.
SHAMAN	Practitioner of a shamanic religion and belief stem.
SITE	Any location inhabited or used by man, where evidences of his activity are to be found
STYLE	An assemblage of rock art which is unified by a set of common techniques and artistic attributes.
STYLIZED	Identifiable forms which have been reduced to abstract forms, such as an oval with an eye to represent a fish or a stick figure with exaggerated horns to represent a mountain sheep.
SUPERIMPOSITION	The placing of one element on top of another. Important in some rock art sites for identifying periods of use and changes in style through time.
ZOOMORPH	In the form of an animal

SAMPLE OF A COMPLETED SITE RECORD

We provide here an example of a reasonably complete site record form, omitting all the photographs, slides, tracings, and other ancillary documentation collected at the site. For brevity, only the documentation on the principal rock art face is given; the site has several other large granite boulders bearing rock art, widely dispersed over a rocky hillside. Also omitted are the regional comparisons and interpretations which would be presented in a comprehensive analysis of the site.

These documents are not presented as an example of a perfect record—the perfect site record is still to be done! They do, however, show an effort to be thorough, complete, and accurate in documenting a rock art site, and few sites in the archives are this well recorded.

This site is also a good example for another reason: the records were made by students, many of whom were recording their first rock art site. The rock art is located near Riverside, in southern California, and is on lands owned by the University of California so that it is accessible to classes on a regular basis. Four classes in rock art recording have now worked at this location, representing a total of well over 100 man-days of recording time. As indicated, not all of that effort is represented in the material presented here, but it does show that substantial time is needed to do all the mapping and recording chores. And this is a small and accessible rock art site which is an easy recording task compared to many rock art sites throughout the world.

While it is valuable to have an example, obviously the specific nature of this record is appropriate to this site but would not be appropriate to other kinds of rock art sites. This is not a model to be followed in a routine way. For each region where rock art is found, it is necessary to develop a recording system that is designed to take into account the regional kinds of rock art. For this reason, Appendix B gives a number of example forms used by rock art recorders in different situations.

The benefits of having this kind of record are obvious: it allows future workers to find the site, and within the site area, the decorated boulders. It provides an inventory of the kind of rock art that is present. This is not, however, a "final report." It needs a more complete motif index: catalog of the rock art elements at the site, as well as a neat, final drawing of the elements and panels showing their relationship to each other. It needs more careful recording of superimpositions (the site has very few). It needs a careful comparison of the similarities and differences among the four decorated areas of the site.

SITE RIV-114, RIVERSIDE COUNTY, CALIFORNIA

Site Survey records from field classes, some directed by C. Meighan and some by JoAnne Van Tilburg.

Site Riv-114. Located on the Motte-Rimrock Reserve. Map: Perris quadrangle (1979, 7.5 minute). UTM grid zone 11, 476,990 E/3, 740,920 N. Township 4S, Range 4W, SW 1/4 of NE 1/4 of NE 1/4 of Section 24.
Property owner: University of California. The site is on lands which are part of the natural lands reserve system of the University; it is administered by the University of California, Riverside, which can grant permission for access. The site area is surrounded by chainlink fence and has a series of grid stakes at 100-meter intervals. The stakes are identified with a letter and a number. A detailed table was constructed showing the compass bearings from the grid stakes to the rock art loci. The primary datum is a 2-inch pipe with a blue top, marked K-16.

Site Riv-114 has four main painted granite boulders bearing red-painted pictographs, distributed on a desert slope covered with similar undecorated boulders. The painted rocks are designated as rock art loci and numbered 2, 3, 4, 5 (see map, fig. A-3)

212

The total record on this site fills several notebooks and includes hundreds of photographs as well as life-size tracings of most of the individual rock art panels. A sample of these records is appended:

Fig. A-1: Original archaeological site record form (from 1979—it has since been
          expanded to include much additional detail)
Fig. A-2: Original rock art record form (also much expanded in later work)
Fig. A-3: Map of site area
Fig. A-4: Map showing relationship of painted boulders to one another
Fig. A-5: Sketch of the appearance of major painted boulder
Fig. A-6: Gridded record form with sketch of the elements on the major painted
          panel of rock art; photo of the same panel is attached to original form.
Fig. A-7: Another panel of rock art at the same site
Fig. A-8: The original summary of elements and frequencies at the site(not the same
          boulders in A-5 to A-7).

SITE No. CA-Riv-114

1. USGS Quad. __Perris, Calif.__ (7½)_____ (15')
2. UTM GRID ZONE 11 __476960__ mE __3740940__ mN
3. Twp. 5-S Range 3-W; ¼of SW ¼of NE ¼of SW ¼of NE of Sec. 24
4. Location At the west end of Lemon street 600 feet, north 250 feet; small stream runs out of canyon with sycamore and pepper trees. Site is at the mouth of this canyon and along the base of boulders.
_____ 5. Contour 1680'
6. Owner __--__ 7. Address __--__
8. Site Description Earlier occupation possible with well defined midden 12 to 30 inches below present surface, with late use indicated by the rock art present.
9. Prehistoric X Ethnographic X Historic _____
10. Area 5 acre area 11. Depth see remarks
12. Vegetation brittlebush, black sage, datura, sycamore, eucaluptus and pepper trees.
13. Water site at mouth of ephemeral stream
14. Site Soil midden present 15. Surrounding Soil decomposing granite boulder outcrops
16. Previous excavation surface collecting in the past, SBC Museum may collection of artifacts from here.
17. Previous site designation, Published references Steward: 1929, 71 Ps., P.90 and Fig.26; SBCM 35; old Penny Ranch, Moymer: 1937, Smith et.al.1976. (Riv-18, Riv-16)
18. Destruction possibility Site is well known, many people know its location. There has no doubt been surface collecting here over the ##
19. Features bedrock mortars, slicks, pictographs.
20. Burials none observed
21. Artifacts little of any cultural remains left on the surface. ## years.Also some earth moving around the base of the hills. There is a well defined midden visible from the stream bed, fire affected rock.
22. Remarks and artifacts washing out. mortars not well defined - 3-4 inch G. Smith may have done some collecting here. There are four panels of rock art, see rock art record forms and site sketch map.
23. Accession # __n/a__ 24. Site Sketch Map yes
25. Date 3 Jan 79 26. Recorder Daniel F. McCarthy 27. Photos yes

A-1 Original archaeological site record form (from 1979—it has since been expanded to include much additional detail)

ROCK ART RECORD

1. Cross Reference Survey Designation Steward 71 Pc; SBCM-35

2. Rock # ___1___   3. Panel or Face # 1

4. Direction of Panel __SE__   5. Kind of Rock __granitic__

6. Dimentions of Decorated Area 2m x 3.5m

7. Method of Decoration: Rock Carving ( ); Rock Painting (X)

8. Colors __red black__   9. Design Elements __hand-__ prints, zoomorphs, abstract crosshatching

10. Superimposition: yes (X); no ( ) __considerable__

11. Degrees of Patination n/a

12. Natural Defacement __some observed but overall, slight__

13. Vandalism __none observed__

14. Associated Site Attributes __see site record__

15. Additional Remarks __Three sketches will be made, one of what__ appears to be the earlist and most faded pigment on rock; 2) later additions-all relatively the same vivid color and presumably the same time period; 3) composite of all elements together in relative positions. This is one of the finest and best preserved sites in southern California.

16. Published References: Specific (X) General ( ) Steward 1929; Moymer 1937; Hoover & Rensch 1945; Smith & Turner 1976.

17. Sketch __yes__   18. Photo NO. Riv-114 Rock #1...
19. Recorded By __Daniel McCarthy__   20. Date 1973, 1979, 1980

A-2   Original rock art record form (also much expanded in later work)

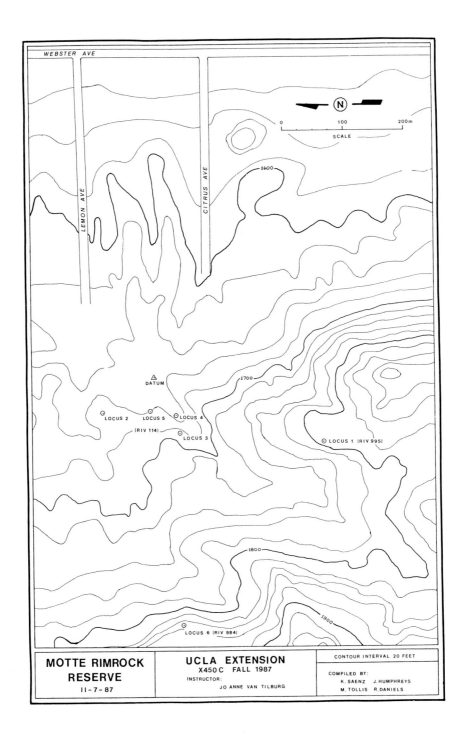

A-3 Map of site area

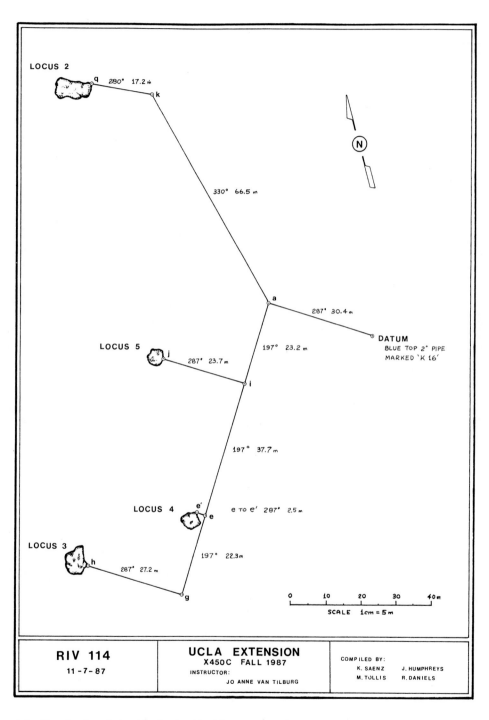

LOCUS 2

q   280° 17.2 m
k
330° 66.5 m
a   287° 30.4 m
DATUM
BLUE TOP 2" PIPE
MARKED 'K 16'

LOCUS 5
j   287° 23.7 m
197° 23.2 m
i
197° 37.7 m

LOCUS 4
e'
e TO e' 287° 2.5 m
e

LOCUS 3
h   287° 27.2 m
197° 22.3 m
g

0   10   20   30   40 m
SCALE 1cm = 5 m

RIV 114 11-7-87	UCLA EXTENSION X450C FALL 1987 INSTRUCTOR: JO ANNE VAN TILBURG	COMPILED BY: K. SAENZ J. HUMPHREYS M. TOLLIS R. DANIELS

A-4   Map showing relationship of painted boulders to one another

217

rock overhang seen from E-SE
peppertree and bushes on the right side

A-5   Sketch of the appearance of major painted boulder

ROCK ART RECORDING FORM

Scale: _____ 1" = 1 ft

Mark which way is up. ↑

Site: RIV 114

Recorder: G. Gallob

Date: 10-12-85

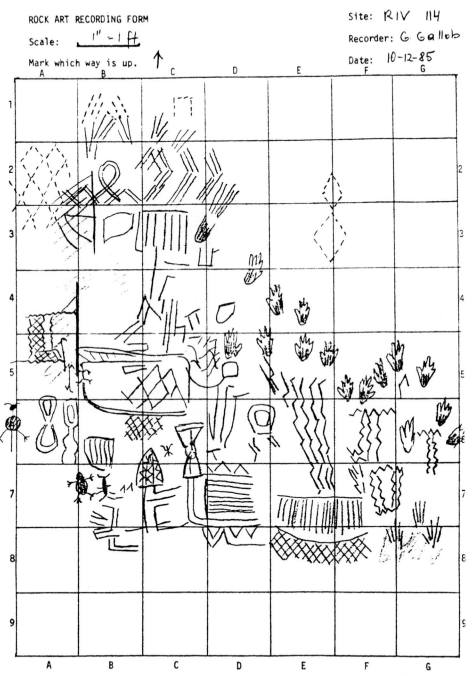

A-6 *Gridded record form with sketch of the elements on the major painted panel of rock art; photo of the same panel is attached to original form.*

Motif Index

crossnatched net   5

right hand   8

left hand   6

drawn hand   5
(2 left, 3 right)

zig -zag line 4

cages   3

chevron   3

elongated fingers   4

hourglass   4

diamond net   6

double zig-zag   1

zig-zag rectangle   4

Single motifs:

butterfly 1

r in
(male?)

field
(female?)

projectile point 1

zoomorphic 2

antropomorphic
4

A-7 Motif index for the previous figure (A-6)

220

MOTIF INDEX DESCRIPTION

I have divided the art on the domed rock into three (3) catagories: abstract curvilinear, abstract linear, and anthropomorphic.

Element Tabulation for Large
Domed Rock at RIV 114

No. in Motif Index	Description	No. of Elements	% of Total
Abstract Curvilinear			
1.	Circular chain ◌◌◌◌	4	7.5%
2.	Connecting links	2	3.7%
3.	Figure 8 (with dots inside)	1.5	2.7%
4.	Large circular design with dots in the middle and a tepee ∧ design at the base	1	1.9%
5.	Connected semi-ovals	1	1.9%
		9.5	17.7%
Abstract Linear			
6.	Diamond elements		
	a. separate	1	1.9%
	b. chain of diamonds (one of which has a dot in the center of each diamond)	2	3.7%
7.	Y design		
	a. separate	8	15.0%
	b. separate upside down	1	1.9%
	c. connected	2	3.7%
	d. connected upside down	1	1.9%
8.	Straight lines	3	6.0%
	a. straight line with 3 wiggly lines connected horizontally to it.	1	1.9%
	b. dots forming a straight line	7	13.0%
9.	Zig-zag lines (unconnected)	2	3.7%
10.	Connected horizontal zig-zag lines	6	11.0%
11.	Connected vertical zig-zag lines	6	11.0%
12.	Dots forming an arrow	1	1.9%
13.	Abstract connecting lines	1	1.9%
14.	A double line X	1	1.9%
		43	80.4%
Anthropomorphic			
15.	Stick figure (human)	1	1.9%
	TOTAL ABSTRACT CURVILINEAR ELEMENTS	9.5	17.7%
	TOTAL ABSTRACT LINEAR ELEMENTS	43.0	80.4%
	TOTAL ANTHROPOMORPHIC ELEMENTS	1.0	1.9%
	TOTAL ELEMENTS	53.5	100.0%

A-8 The original summary of elements and frequencies at the site (not the same boulders in A-5 to A-7).

APPENDIX B

RECORDING FORMS

The following pages provide a sampling of forms used in rock art recording tasks. No attempt has been made to include all possible record forms—there are probably as many of these as there are rock art recorders. Depending on the site and the nature of the rock art, you may want to customize your own recording form, using those included here only as a source of ideas. A general form which allows space for every conceivable variety of rock art is not relevant to the individual site, which will reveal only a small fraction of rock art possibilities. You do not want to fill out a lot of blanks which are not relevant to your site. For example, if your site contains only petroglyphs and no painted elements, you don't want a lot of blanks on your recording form asking for details of paint color. Your form should include only the traits and features appropriate to your site, and whenever possible use "check-off boxes" instead of blanks which have to be filled out one by one. For example, to indicate the paint colors, rather than providing a space to write in the colors, why not provide check boxes:

Red ☐

White ☐

Black ☐

Other ☐ _____

You may, of course, want to be more precise and record Munsell colors, shades of red, or whatever, but this information can also be condensed into check boxes. This simple approach will greatly shorten the time needed to fill out forms. In situations where a crew of several people is doing the recording, use of check boxes also insures that standard responses will be made and that individual crew members will not forget to include some part of the data.

The main value of any form is as a check-list, reminding the recorder of observations to be made. On the other hand, if the form does not include everything relevant to the site, it is easy for recorders to fail to note other information that may be even more important than the check-list. This is why the crew chief needs to design the forms for the specific site, so that the key data are collected and essential observations are made. Even with the best of forms, however, the crew chief needs his own notebook and his own search for additional data (not on the forms) which ought to be included in the description of the site.

Although it is desirable, and often essential, to design your own forms so that they are compatible with the particular site you are recording, it is also very desirable to develop records that are compatible with the records of central recording agencies such as state siterecords, usually maintained by the State Historic Preservation Office, or records maintained by universities and museums. Since most agencies are computerizing their data base, it will be easier for them to make effective use of your recording effort if you have done it in their style. If you know that copies of your records will go to a central repository, you can ask for the forms used by the repository and use those as a basic record. It may be that you can design a supplementary form, specific to your site, and add that to whatever "standard" forms you decide to use.

UNIVERSITY OF CALIFORNIA ARCHAEOLOGICAL SURVEY

PETROGLYPH RECORD

1. Site _____   2. Cross Reference Survey Record _____

3. Face _____   4. Dimensions of Decorated Area _____

5. Horizontal location _____

6. Kind of Rock _____

7. Position of Rock _____

8. Method of Decoration: Pecked ( ); rubbed grooves ( ); painted ( ); other ( )

9. Colors _____

10. Design elements _____

    _____

    _____

11. Superimposition _____

12. Natural Defacement _____

13. Vandalism _____

14. Associated Features _____

15. Additional Remarks _____

    _____

    _____

    _____

    _____

    _____

    _____

16. Published References _____

    _____

17. Sketch _____   18. Scale of sketch _____

19. Photo Nos. _____

20. Recorded by _____   21. Date _____

ROCK ART RECORD FORM

LOCATION
    Site Name_____ Site No._____State____
    County_____Section_____ Twp._____Range_____
    Map Source_____ Date of map_____
    Location Discription_____
    _____Accessibility:Foot_____Sedan____4-wh Dr__
    Ownership_____
    Attitude toward recording_____

SITE
    Site description_____
    _____
    Situation: bedrock_____cave_____boulder_____cliff_____other_____
    Rock type: granite____basalt____sandstone____tuff____other_____
    Dimensions of: site_____ decorated area_____
    Technique: painted____pecked____grooved____incised____other____
    Colors (if painted) _____
    Describe design elements_____
    _____
    Deterioration: natural_____vandalism_____
    Direction art faces_____
    Cultural features nearby (ruins, artifacts, etc.)_____
    _____
    Natural resources (water, vegetation, etc.)_____
    _____

RECORDING
    No. of photos taken: color slide_____B/W_____Other_____
    No. of drawings_____scale drawings_____
    Other recording methods used _____
    Additional notes_____
    _____
    _____
    Sources of information for site_____
    _____

    Please sketch site and some design elements on the back of this form.

    Recorded by _____ Date_____
    Address_____Phone_____

PETROGLYPH RECORD

Petroglyph record no. _____ Site _____ Date _____ Recorder _____

No. of decorated faces: _____ Dimensions of decorated area(s): A. _____

Kind of rock: B. _____

                                                                                                            C. _____
Superimposition:
                                                                                                            D. _____

Natural weathering:

Vandalism:

Associated cultural remains:

Published references:

DESIGN ELEMENTS

METHOD OF DECORATION

☐ Pecked
☐ Rubbed grooves
☐ Painted
☐ Other (specify):

COLORS

☐ Red
☐ Black
☐ White
☐ Yellow
☐ Other (specify):

FACE:

Scale

Photographs taken ?

Indicate north

ROCK ART RECORD

UCLA Rock Art Archive

Site Number_____   County_____
USGS Quad_____ 7.5'   Latitude_____
            _____ 15'   Longitude_____
UTMG Grid_____ Calif. Coordinates_____
Twp._____Range_____   _____1/4 of _____1/4 _____ of Section _____

LOCATION DESCRIPTION: (Road directions; orient by compass).

SITE DESCRIPTION:

Cave shelter_____Exposed rock_____Other_____
Indicate direction rock art faces_____
Dimensions of decorated area(s)_____Kind of rock_____
Method of decoration_____Colors_____
Design elements:

Superimposition_____Natural defacement_____Vandalism _____
Associated features_____
Ownership_____
Attitude toward recording_____
Published references_____
Recorded by_____
Address_____Date_____
Photo record_____
Additional remarks:

Sketch: (Use reverse if necessary. Include general sketch of shelter or rock indicating panel locations and their directions).

ROCK ART SURVEY RECORD
To be attached to the SITE RECORD form

31. Site Number:...
    UTM Coord:...
    USGS Quad:..
    Twnshp:.............;Range:..............;Sec:..............

32. Usual Site Name:...

33. Indicate best approach to this site:..
    ....
    ....

34. Brief site description (attach site survey or sketch and label rock art panels with capital letters):............................
    ....

    a. ☐ Habitation Site; ☐ Hunting Camp Site; ☐ Gathering Site; ☐ ....
    b. (Attach): ☐ Geology of Site; ☐ Vegetation Description; ☐ Building Description; ☐ Artifacts, etc.
    c. Outlook view from site (attach slides/photos/sketches):..
    ....;

    Compass Directions of note:...

35. Description of the rock art panels and their location(s) on the site (utilizing the capital letter ID of the sketch--34)
    ....
    ....
    ....
    ....

36. Listing of rock art elements (use arabic numbers to identify each element, indicate condition under comment):

Panel Letter	Element Number	Color Identification (Munsell Chart)	Sketch Yes/No	Slide/Photo Yes / No	Tracing Yes/No	Comment and Condition of the Element and Rock
....	....	....	☐ ☐	☐ ☐	☐ ☐	....
....	....	....	☐ ☐	☐ ☐	☐ ☐	....
....	....	....	☐ ☐	☐ ☐	☐ ☐	....
....	....	....	☐ ☐	☐ ☐	☐ ☐	....
....	....	....	☐ ☐	☐ ☐	☐ ☐	....
....	....	....	☐ ☐	☐ ☐	☐ ☐	....
....	....	....	☐ ☐	☐ ☐	☐ ☐	....
....	....	....	☐ ☐	☐ ☐	☐ ☐	....
....	....	....	☐ ☐	☐ ☐	☐ ☐	....
....	....	....	☐ ☐	☐ ☐	☐ ☐	....
....	....	....	☐ ☐	☐ ☐	☐.☐	....

Please continue listing of the elements on the backside of this form.

37. Overall presentday rock art condition:.............................; Destruction Possibility:..........................

38. a. Ownership of the site:..............................; Address:...................................
    ....Phone:..........................; ....ZIP..............
    b. Access to site is obtained from:..............................Phone: ....

39. Previous reports on this site (if known):..............................
    a. Archaeological Information, including rock art:..............................
    b. Ethnographic Information:..............................

40. This rock art survey is made by:..............................; Date:..........................
    Address:..............................; Phone:..........................
    City, State:..............................; Mail Code/ZIP:..........................

    Location at which primary records (or copies) are available:..............................
    PLEASE USE THE BACK OF THIS PAGE FOR ADDITIONAL INFORMATION AND YOUR COMMENTS:

A copy of this report should be sent to the Archaeological Survey Clearance Center in the geographic area of the site.
A list of Archaeological Survey Clearance Centers may be found in the "Rock Art Recording Manual" (UCLA 1979)
LAMC (Rev 12-79) Arch/Anth:4

EQUIPMENT LIST

Esther Schwartz

The following can serve as a checklist of supplies which are used in the recording of rock art sites. Some of these supplies are essential, while others are merely useful and may make the recording task easier.

INDIVIDUAL RECORDING EQUIPMENT

- **Clip board** to hold forms. Some clip boards for field use are made as shallow boxes of plastic or metal, allowing forms and writing supplies to be kept inside. These also have the advantage of being sealable so that dust and moisture can be kept off the record forms once they are completed.
- **Pencils**, several soft lead (no. 2), and a small pencil sharpener or knife.
- **Pens**, nylon or other hard tip, black. Be sure that they are new ones or have not been left open so that the tips are dried out. For special purposes, it may be desirable to have colored pens (red, yellow, etc.) but the initial field records should be done in black so that they can be clearly reproduced on a copying machine—some colors are faint or absent when copied on Xerox or similar copiers.
- **Eraser**, "Pink Pearl" or Eberhard Faber kneaded rubber
- **Pocket compass**
- **Three-meter metal tape measure** with belt clip, self-closing
- **Straight edge or ruler**, 6 or 12 inch, also marked in metric system
- **Rubber bands**, large, to hold forms on clip board in windy weather
- **Paper clips**, including some large ones
- **Magnifying glass**, small but strong
- **Line level**, to attach to string reference lines so that they can be made horizontal
- **String grids**, 20 cm. and 10 cm. squares, with masking tape to attach them.

If string grids are not used, a ball of strong nylon cord which can be used to provide reference lines for drawings.

- **Camera** and supply of appropriate film
- **Recording paper** includes:

Blank paper for notes (or a small pocket notebook)

Graph paper for recording—use decimal-gridded paper (e.g. large units divided into 10 rather than 12 smaller units). Ordinarily paper gridded 10 units to the inch is satisfactory. Graph paper that is too fine (1 mm. squares, for example) is more difficult to use. Be sure the graph paper is printed in blue lines that will disappear in photographic reproduction; this is "Fade out" or "Clear print" graph paper. Do not use graph paper printed in orange or other colors since the grid will print black when it is photographed or copied, becoming very obtrusive and interfering with the drawing.

Printed recording forms: site record forms and whatever forms are being used for rock art recording and tabulation.

TEAM SUPPLIES

Most rock art recording is not done solo but involves a small group of people working together. The crew chief should bring along a full set of supplies to back up the individuals who forgot some critical item (such as recording forms or a tape measure). In addition, the team may find it very valuable to have the following:

- **Binoculars**
- **String,** large rolls for staking out mapping lines. Strong nylon twine sold in builders' supply houses is ideal; some workers prefer the bright yellow variety since it is more visible and helps people to avoid tripping over strings.
- **Wooden stakes,** at least a dozen, for string lines and marking mapping points (garden supply or lumber yard).
- **Long tape measure** (30 meters)
- **Brushes** for lightly cleaning rock surfaces: tooth brushes or paint brushes
- **First aid kit:** band-aids, antiseptic, tweezers, etc.
- **Insect repellent** and sometimes insecticide if the area proves to be infested with ants, wasps.
- **Extra site record forms,** petroglyph record forms, and graph paper for drawings
- **Extra pens, pencils, marker pens.** Colored pens and/or pencils
- **"Office supplies"**India ink or disposable India ink pen. A paper punch.
- **Scissors**

231

- **Plastic sheets** for making tracings.
- **Cotton cloth** for rubbings, several yards (old sheets may provide good cloth for this purpose, but some people prefer to use cloth which is approximately the same color as the rock)
- **Wax** (used for shoe heels; get it at shoe repair shops) or shoe polish brush and paste shoe polish. These are for making rubbings
- **Masking tape** or **duct tape**
- **Pruning shears** or garden clippers (to cut away obscuring vegetation and plant roots)
- **Ropes and ladders** may be essential in some sites. Even a small step-ladder can be a great help in getting a good vantage point on some rock art, both for drawings and photography.

PERSONAL AND "SURVIVAL" EQUIPMENT

- **Backpack,** small and lightweight to carry all your gear. Nylon, water-repellent fabric is excellent for this purpose.
- **Weather protection.** In some areas light rain coats are needed. More common is the need for protection from excess sun and heat: sun glasses, sun lotion, and a sun hat. The sunlight bouncing off the rocks at a rock art site can be intense.
- **Plastic bags** to protect your records, camera, and other gear from dust and moisture. For small items, zip-lock plastic bags are good, but you may also want to carry a couple of large "garbage bags" to cover up everything in case of rain or dusty conditions. They can also be used to carry out whatever trash results from your activities: paper scraps, lunch bags, and beverage containers. Use the lighter-colored bags—the black ones collect a lot of heat and are not good for cameras or film.
- **Flashlight** (and extra batteries), can help in observing the rock art by illuminating dark corners and side-lighting petroglyphs.
- **Canteen**
- **Communication device** if you are going to be working at a distance from everyone else. The simplest is a whistle or other noise maker. A walkie-talkie is ideal. Consider that a minor fall or sprained ankle can put you in the position of needing help, and it may be long in appearing if you are off in the middle of a desert somewhere.
- **Personal toiletries** and minor first aid supplies. In desert areas, for example, one might consider carrying small pointed-nose pliers for the removal of the inevitable cactus spines, and maybe a snake-bite kit if you are in a rocky area known for snakes as well as rock-art enthusiasts. Pocket knife? Toilet paper? Chapstick? Sunburn lotion?

APPENDIX D
CODE OF ETHICS: ARARA

The American Rock Art Association (ARARA) adopted a code of ethics in 1987 (printed in La Pintura, 14:1, 3). This brief statement is reproduced here as a guide to the responsibilities of workers at rock art sites. The text of this volume offers a number of other guidelines which are common sense suggestions, but the ethics statement of ARARA deals specifically with potential damage to the rock art and to the archaeological remains which are sometimes associated.

1. All local, state and national antiquities laws will be strictly adhered to by the membership of ARARA. Rock art research will be subject to appropriate regulations of property access requirements.

2. All rock art recording shall be nondestructive with regard to the rock art itself and the associated archaeological remains which may be present. No artifacts shall be collected unless the work is done as part of a legally constituted program of archaeological survey or excavation.

3. No excavation shall be conducted unless the work is done as part of a legally constituted excavation project. Removal of soil shall not be undertaken for the sole purpose of exposing subsurface rock art.

4. Potentially destructive recording and research procedures shall be undertaken only after careful consideration of any possible damage to the rock art site.
5. Use of the name of the American Rock Art Research Association, the initials of A.R.A.R.A. and/or logos adopted by the association and the identification of an

individual as a member of ARARA are allowed only in conjunction with rock art projects undertaken in full accordance with accepted professional archaeological standards. The ARARA name may not be used for commercial purposes. While members may use their affiliation with ARARA for identification purposes, research projects may not be represented as having the sponsorship of ARARA without express approval of the Executive Committee.

These provisions adopted by ARARA are printed on the membership cards and failure to observe them is cause for exclusion from membership. They are equally appropriate for all other organized groups. The first four provisions are designed to protect the resource (rock art and associated features). The last one is designed to protect the name and reputation of the research group. This is important because individuals sometimes misrepresent their connections with organizations, museums, and universities in order to gain access to sites and permission to carry out their work. If you are doing a project sponsored or supported by an organized research unit, be sure to carry a letter identifying you and your association with that unit.

BOCK'S LAWS OF ROCK ART RECORDING

Frank Bock

GENERAL LAWS

1.   No matter how remote the rock art panel, you will find an empty box of Kodachrome 64 on the ground.

2.   If a recording team, headed by a Ph.D. with 25 years experience in recording rock art, spends one month at one panel, 75% of the photographs will be blurred.

First corollary: The youngest child of the newest member of the team (who is there because no baby sitter could be found) will produce the best photographs, all taken with an instamatic camera.

Second corollary: This child will not part with the photos since he/she plans to share them at show-and-tell at school.

3.   After travelling 50 miles to the site from base camp, over four-wheel drive terrain, the surveyor will realize he left transit, tripod, and plane-table back at camp.

First corollary: The surveyor, using his watch as a compass and relying on Boy Scout reckoning, will draw a map which is irretrievably in error.

Second corollary: When a second professional surveyor is hired—at an expense equal to the entire project—*then* the original surveyor's map will be found to be accurate within 0.005%. When the final report is written, the map once again will be found to be irretrievably in error.

Third corollary: When the final report is written, the map once again will be found to be irretrievably in error.

4.   The photographic crew, using their own cameras, will have complete lapses of memory and forget how to use them.

First corollary: At least two rolls of film per week will not be threaded properly in the camera, producing 72 blank frames.

Second corollary: Twelve percent of all pictures taken will include a thumb.

Third corollary: Six percent of all pictures taken will be snapped as the crew member climbs over rocks, falls down, sways on top of a ladder, or sees a cute animal or flower.

5.   Seventeen percent of the time spent at each rock art panel will be spent in arguing over what is and what is not a petroglyph.

First corollary: This disagreement will lead to 18% of all photos taken to include rock scars, exfoliation, and other forms of natural marking.

Second corollary: All of these photos will be labelled "random pecking" or "unidentifiable pecking."

6.   The local amateur archaeological society will plan to visit the recording team on the first day before anyone on the team knows what he or she is doing.

First corollary: Five of these visitors, who will have never seen rock art before, will proceed to tell the crew how to record the site and what they are doing wrong.

Second corollary: Four of the visitors, bored with watching, will explain how they have worked on *real* archaeological digs in Israel and South America.

Third corollary: The datum, baseline, section poles, element numbers, and a considerable number of survey stakes will be trampled, broken, or displaced by this eager group when they break for lunch.

7.   When the local residents hear what is happening, the one person who can read rock art will visit the site.

First corollary: This resident, who goes by the nickname of "Ol' Pops," will corner each crew member and tell his story of how his grandaddy homesteaded near here over a hundred years ago.

Second corollary: Ol' Pops will read the rock art relating it to the bible, the Egyptian *Book of the Dead,* and /or ancient Sumerian writings.

Third corollary: Ol' Pops will point out a petroglyph of a map showing where Montezuma's treasure is buried. He relates this with great authority since he has been there and seen it.

8. On the last day of recording, due to different lighting conditions, at least fifteen petroglyphs that were not recorded will be discovered.

First corollary: This discovery will be made by Ol' Pops, who knew they were there all along, but wanted to test the capabilities of the recording crew.

Second corollary: In order not to dig out all the recording equipment, that has been packed away for the return trip, the leader will ascertain that all fifteen elements are "modern scratching, made with a steel rock pick."

9. When the recording is finished it will take the leader two years to write the report.

First corollary: The editor will garble most of the text, mislabel five of the illustrations, and put his name first in the credits.

Second corollary: By the time the scientific journal report on the site is published, a coffee-table publication replete with color plates and fantasized interpretations will have been marketed.

[Reproduced with permission from La Pintura, Vol. 15, Nos. 1 and 2, p. 18].

ABOUT THE AUTHORS

Kay Kenady Sanger is an archaeologist and writer who began photographing rock art while living in Australia in 1969. Since then, she has recorded rock art in Costa Rica, Easter Island, Mexico, and Sweden, as well as the western United States. She has taught classes on rock art and California Indians to adults and children in southern California for the past 10 years, and she is chair of the Publications Committee of the American Rock Art Research Association.

Clement Meighan is an archaeologist and professor of anthropology at the University of California, Los Angeles. He has published papers and monographs on rock art subjects and has recorded rock art sites in many countries on four continents. In addition to organizing and teaching classes on recording and analysis of prehistoric rock art, since 1978 he has directed the Rock Art Archive (part of the Institute of Archaeology) at U.C.L.A. This is the first organized research facility in North America to concentrate exclusively on rock art research.